CAREER CHOICES
for Students of
✦
ECONOMICS

by
CAREER ASSOCIATES

Walker and Company
NEW YORK

First published in the United States of America in 1985 by the Walker Publishing Company, Inc.

Published simultaneously in Canada by John Wiley & Sons Canada, Limited, Rexdale, Ontario.

Library of Congress Cataloging in Publication Data
Main entry under title:

Career choices for students of economics.

  Bibliography: p.
  1. United States—Occupations. 2. College graduates—Employment—United States. 3. Vocational guidance—United States. I. Career Associates.
HF5382.5.U5C2553   1985   331.7'023   83-40443
ISBN 0-8027-0792-0
ISBN 0-8027-7249-8 (pbk.)

Printed in the United States of America

10 9 8 7 6 5 4 3 2 1

Titles In The Series

Career Choices For Students Of:
Art
Business
Communications and Journalism
Computer Science
Economics
English
History
Mathematics
Political Science and Government
Psychology

Career Choices For Undergraduates Considering:
Law
An M.B.A.

Acknowledgments

We gratefully acknowledge the help of the many people who spent time talking to our research staff about employment opportunities in their fields. This book would not have been possible without their assistance. Our thanks, too, to Catalyst, which has one of the best career libraries in the country in its New York, NY, offices, and to the National Society for Internships and Experiential Education, Raleigh, NC, which provided information on internship opportunities for a variety of professions.

CAREER ASSOCIATES

CONTENTS

WHAT'S IN THIS BOOK FOR YOU?

Recent college graduates, no matter what their major has been, too often discover that there is a dismaying gap between their knowledge and planning and the reality of an actual career. Possibly even more unfortunate is the existence of potentially satisfying careers that graduates do not even know about. Although advice from campus vocational counselors, family, friends, and fellow students can be extremely helpful, there is no substitute for a structured exploration of the various alternatives open to graduates.

The Career Choices Series was created to provide you with the means to conduct such an exploration. It gives you specific, up-to-date information about the entry-level job opportunities in a variety of industries relevant to your degree and highlights opportunities that might otherwise be overlooked. Through its many special features—such as sections on internships, qualifications, and working conditions—the Career Choices Series can help you find out where your interests and abilities lie in order to point your search for an entry-level job in a productive direction. This book cannot find you a job—only you can provide the hard work, persistence, and ingenuity that that requires—but it can save you valuable time and energy. By helping you to narrow the range of your search to careers that are truly suitable for you, this book can help make hunting for a job an exciting adventure rather than a dreary—and sometimes frightening—chore.

The book's easy-to-use format combines general information about each of the industries covered with the hard facts that job-hunters must have. An overall explanation of each industry is followed by authoritative material on the job outlook for entry-level candidates, the competition for the openings that exist, and the new opportunities that may arise from such factors as expansion and technological development. There is a listing of employers by type and by geographic location and a sampling of leading companies by name—by no means all, but enough to give you a good idea of who the employers are.

The section on how to break into the field is not general how-to-get-a-job advice, but rather zeroes in on ways of getting a foot in the door of a particular industry.

You will find the next section, a description of the major functional areas within each industry, especially valuable in making your initial job choice. For example, communications majors aiming for magazine work can evaluate the editorial end, advertising space sales, circulation, or production. Those interested in accounting are shown the differences between management, government, and public accounting. Which of the various areas described offers you the best chance of an entry-level job? What career paths are likely to follow from that position? Will they help you reach your ultimate career goal? The sooner you have a basis to make the decision, the better prepared you can be.

For every industry treated and for the major functional areas within that industry, you'll learn what your duties—both basic and more challenging—are likely to be, what hours you'll work, what your work environment will be, and what range of salary to expect.* What personal and professional qualifications must you have? How can you move up—and to what? This book tells you.

You'll learn how it is possible to overcome the apparent contradiction of the truism, "To get experience you have to have experience." The kinds of extracurricular activities and work experience—summer and/or part-time—that can help you get and perform a job in your chosen area are listed. Internships are another way to get over that hurdle, and specific information is included for each industry. But you should also know that the directories published by the National Society for Internships and Experiential Education (Second Floor, 124 St. Mary's Street, Raleigh, NC 27605) are highly detailed and very useful. They are: *Directory of Undergraduate Internships, Directory of Washington Internships,* and *Directory of Public Service Internships.*

You'll find a list of the books and periodicals you should read to keep up with the latest trends in an industry you are considering, and the names and addresses of professional associations that can be helpful to you—through student chapters, open meetings, and

---

* Salary figures given are the latest available as the book goes to press.

printed information. Finally, interviews with professionals in each field bring you the experiences of people who are actually working in the kinds of jobs you may be aiming for.

Although your entry-level job neither guarantees nor locks you into a lifelong career path, the more you know about what is open to you, the better chance you'll have for a rewarding work future. The information in these pages will not only give you a realistic basis for a good start, it will help you immeasurably in deciding what to explore further on your own. So good reading, good hunting, good luck, and the best of good beginnings.

ACCOUNTING

PENCILS, ledger books, endless columns of figures—a career spent with the tools of the accounting profession appeals to many business majors. With tax laws becoming more complicated and government regulations requiring more careful audits, the skills of the accountant are now more in demand than ever before. Accountants design, maintain, and audit the financial records of businesses and institutions. They aid management personnel in financial planning and ensure the accuracy of all financial statements. The accountant makes a strong contribution to an organization's credibility in the eyes of investors, creditors, government agencies (particularly in regard to taxes), trade and professional association members, and contributors.

A business administration graduate with a strong background in accounting has as good a chance of entering the profession as a graduate who holds an accounting degree. Many employers look favorably on the business administration major because it gives students an understanding of basic business functions.

Obviously, fiscal and mathematical skills are of the highest importance, but prospective employers look for much more in a

job candidate. Accountants do not work over their books in soli-
tude; they are active participants in daily business operations.
Their findings and observations must be used by others, so the
would-be accountant must have exceptional organizational and
communications skills. For this reason, a well-rounded liberal arts
education can be an asset. Continuing to learn is also a vital part of
any accounting career because of ever changing tax laws and
business regulations. Further education can also open up new
career possibilities as your growing knowledge and experience
allow you to explore new options.

Accounting professionals work in three major areas:

- **Public Accounting**
- **Management Accounting**
- **Government Accounting**

Public accounting is the most visible branch of the industry,
primarily because of the status of the Certified Public Accountant
(C.P.A.). Public accountants serve client businesses by auditing
their books, preparing tax returns, and advising on tax, business,
investment, and related concerns. Management accountants, also
known as private, internal, or industrial accountants, work within
industries and businesses and with charitable, educational, and
religious institutions. They handle such functions as cost analysis,
budgeting, payroll, and inventory control, and offer advice on
financial matters. Government accountants perform the same role,
but work within the government rather than in private industry.
    Public accounting firms hire the majority of recent
graduates—well over one-half—yet more accountants are employed by private industry than by any other type of employer.
This disparity exists because private industry draws experienced
accountants out of public and government accounting.
    Information processing technologies have significantly affected
the daily routines of many accounting professionals. Computers

are increasingly relied on for record-keeping and financial analysis. Accountants are now able to complete many jobs more quickly without sacrificing standards of thoroughness and accuracy.

Job Outlook

Job Openings Will Grow: Faster than average

Competition for Jobs: Keen

Most entry-level jobs are found in public accounting firms, although recent graduates will also find openings in management and government accounting. Because of current hiring cutbacks, expect the stiffest competition when applying to the federal government.

New Job Opportunities: Tax work has always been an important part of accounting, but the expanding body of tax law now confronting businesses is producing an increased demand for tax accountants. Experience with the Internal Revenue Service (IRS) is certainly the best means of beginning a tax accounting career, but jobs in public and management accounting can also involve the newcomer in a great deal of tax work.

Geographic Job Index

New York, NY, Chicago, IL, Los Angeles, CA, and Washington, DC, have higher concentrations of accountants than other specific locales, but jobs are not limited to these cities. Accounting jobs may be found in all regions of the United States, mainly in urban and industrial areas.

Who the Employers Are

PUBLIC ACCOUNTING for one of the 30,000 U.S. public accounting firms can mean working in a small, one-person operation or for an international giant employing thousands. The largest are the so-called Big Eight, which have the personnel to handle major corporations as clients and, as a result, great prestige.

MANAGEMENT ACCOUNTING in many businesses may require only one person handling some accounting functions, but the real career opportunities lie in firms large enough to have a formal accounting department. Jobs exist in both manufacturing and service industries.

GOVERNMENT employs accounting staffs in departments and agencies at the federal, state, county, and municipal levels; smaller governmental units, such as townships and boroughs, often hire public accounting firms to handle their books.

Major Employers

THE BIG EIGHT

> Arthur Andersen & Company, Chicago IL
> Arthur Young & Company, New York, NY
> Coopers & Lybrand, New York, NY
> Deloitte, Haskins & Sells, New York, NY
> Ernst & Whinney, Cleveland, OH
> Peat, Marwick, Mitchell & Company, New York, NY
> Price Waterhouse & Company, New York, NY
> Touche Ross & Company, New York, NY

These companies have branches throughout the country.

GOVERNMENT departments employing the largest numbers of accountants and auditors are:

> Department of Agriculture
> Department of Defense Audit Agencies
> Department of Energy
> Department of Health and Human Services
> Department of the Air Force
> Department of the Army
> Department of the Navy
> General Accounting Office
> Treasury Department (includes the Internal Revenue
> > Service)

How to Break into the Field

Because of keen competition for jobs with the Big Eight, you need a strong grade point average and a high class standing in order to be considered for an entry-level position. These firms recruit heavily on selected college campuses, as do other large employers of public accountants. However, because most public accounting firms do not have recruitment personnel, your best bet is to make your own investigation through personal referrals and newspaper advertisements.

Large businesses also recruit entry-level management accountants, and on-campus interviews are a good way to find out more about the wide opportunities in this area. Again, keep an eye on the classified ads and make direct applications to companies that interest you.

You must apply for government accounting jobs in the same way as for any other government job. At the federal level, contact the nearest job information center for application details. Most federal applicants must go through the Office of Personnel Management, but some departments, such as the Department of Defense, have their own personnel offices. In either case, you must submit the standard federal application form, SF-171, and a college transcript. Accounting majors are preferred for accounting positions, but business majors with 24 semester hours of accounting and auditing courses are equally eligible. After your application is received, your qualifications are evaluated and you are given a numerical rating. When your number reaches the head of a list of qualified candidates for the position that interests you, you will be interviewed. If the job is in another part of the country and you are willing to relocate—always an important consideration when applying for federal work—you may be interviewed on the phone. The entry-level rating for college graduates on the federal pay schedule is either GS-5 or GS-7. You are rated at a higher level if you have an exceptional academic record or a year of work experience at the time you apply. Your application with the federal government remains active as long as you report any relevant work experience within 10 to 12 months.

Application requirements with smaller government bodies vary.

Contact state, county, or local government personnel agencies to learn their needs for entry-level accountants and the requirements.

International Job Opportunities

The largest public accounting firms and corporations have overseas branches, but these are staffed by foreign nationals in most areas. An exception is the Middle East, where Americans who are fluent in Arabic are needed.

PUBLIC ACCOUNTING

The most important function of the public accountant is auditing. This includes an inspection of the client's internal operations, records and documents, and, possibly, company employees on the job. The auditor inspects procedures for bill paying, inventory control, and other financial operations and establishes the balances of income, debits, assets, and investments. Auditors base their final reports on their observations, experience, and knowledge of sound business practices. A background in economics and business administration is valuable in this respect. Auditors must also be able to exercise good judgment.

The audit gives clients a complete and accurate assessment of their financial standing; it aids management in planning and protects investors and stockholders. An annual audit is mandatory for all publicly held corporations.

Many businesses and organizations, even those with internal accounting departments, hire public accountants to prepare tax returns. These clients see a distinct advantage in having an objective agency perform this important task. In such cases, the public accountant adopts the role of tax adviser.

Some businesses also engage public accountants to provide advice on investments and accounting procedures, performing for small firms the same functions as internal accountants in larger businesses.

Certified public accountants receive greater recognition than other public accountants, both from the public and from other accounting professionals. You are awarded certification once you have demonstrated your mastery of accounting skills in a five-part examination. The exam tests accounting theory, commercial law, and accounting techniques. A standard national test is used, but it is administered by state boards of accountancy, which may set their own requirements. All sections of the test need not be taken in one sitting, and sections not passed may be retaken. But the time period in which you must pass the complete exam varies from state to state. Some states also require a minimum amount of work experience as a public accountant before awarding the certificate. To check the standards of the state in which you plan to practice, consult that state's board of accountancy or the American Institute of Certified Public Accountants (AICPA).

To begin preparing for the exam while still in school, pay particular attention to courses in accounting theory. This material is learned only in an academic environment; many C.P.A.s recommend that this section be taken first, before your classroom knowledge is obscured by time.

The advantages of holding the C.P.A. are many; it serves as tangible proof of your skill and your commitment to the profession. Public accounting firms, particularly the largest, often expect their accountants to receive certification as quickly as state law allows.

Beyond the entry level, the C.P.A. is often a requirement for advancement. Employers, even those in management and government accounting, prefer to see a C.P.A. when hiring an individual with public accounting experience. In private industry, C.P.A.s tend to be better paid than their noncertified counterparts. Although a varied career is possible without the certificate, having it opens a multitude of otherwise unavailable opportunities.

Your experience at the entry level will vary significantly depending on the size of the public accounting firm. In the Big Eight, you will undergo a brief training period—generally a few weeks— to acquaint yourself with your employer's standards and practices. Staff accountants are closely supervised and generally work as teams; because of the size of corporate accounts, these teams may only handle a single area of a much larger account. Although this arrangement may sound limiting, large accounting firms provide well-rounded experience by rotating their entry-level personnel. This rotation system allows you to observe all aspects of an audit.

Junior accountants in smaller firms gain a different sort of experience. They are generally less closely supervised and they work as assistants to senior accountants. As an entry-level accountant in a smaller firm, you will have the opportunity to see an entire account in depth. You will learn the inner workings of client businesses and build personal relationships with clients to an extent rarely possible at large organizations.

Qualifications

Personal: Good concentration. Patience. Accuracy and attention to detail. Flexibility. Objectivity. Ability to judge and make decisions. Reliability.

Professional: Writing and communications skills. Exceptional mathematical ability. Commitment to professional standards. Ability to work independently.

Career Paths

LEVEL	JOB TITLE	EXPERIENCE NEEDED
Entry	Staff or junior accountant	College degree
2	Senior accountant	3-4 years
3	Manager	5-7 years
4	Partner	8+ years

Job Responsibilities

Entry Level

THE BASICS: Going over a client's books. Performing transactional tests (these verify the accuracy of bookkeeping procedures). Preparing tax returns.

MORE CHALLENGING DUTIES: Offering your recommendations and opinions on sections of an audit to senior personnel. Doing background research. Learning tax law. Meeting with clients.

Moving Up

Promotion in any size firm depends on your competence in accounting techniques and procedures. Senior accountants are responsible for the transactional tests that ensure the accuracy of your findings. At the entry level you may be asked your opinion of an audit's findings, but only experienced personnel report directly to a client. Managers oversee the largest audits and service clients. The partners are the owners/executives of a public accounting firm, and are ultimately responsible for all decisions concerning the firm and its clients. They also solicit new accounts. You must be invited to become a partner and, in some cases, may have to buy into the firm.

In a small firm, your advancement to a high level of responsibility may be quick, but many accountants advance faster by switching firms. In the Big Eight, a large number of staff accountants leave after approximately three to five years. Usually these individuals have not been promoted as quickly as they would like. Their frustration is understandable when you consider that only 2 percent of incoming staff accountants make it to the level of partner.

Solo practice is an option open to experienced accountants. The advantage of working alone or starting your own small firm is that you may be selective in your choice of accounts. However, only a highly organized individual can successfully handle solo practice.

MANAGEMENT ACCOUNTING

Management accountants handle internal financial record-keeping; provide data on investments, taxes, budgets, and cost analysis; and aid executive personnel in financial decision-making. These duties sound similar to those of public accountants with good reason—many businesses employ public accountants only to conduct audits; in-house staff handle all other accounting functions. Other organizations divide their accounting needs between public and management accounting, giving some functions, such as taxes, to an outside firm and assigning day-to-day jobs, such as payroll and budgeting, to the internal staff. For this reason, the career paths and duties of management accountants vary considerably.

The general accounting department handles daily business needs, such as payroll, budgeting, accounts receivable, accounts payable, general ledger, and financial statements. In smaller firms, the title general accountant might be held by the individual who handles or directs most or all accounting functions. This individual would, in turn, work most closely with public accountants if the organization employs them.

General accountants must pay close attention to all laws and regulations affecting daily business operations. They are involved in sending out all payments, royalties, dividends, rents, and other necessary expenditures. General accountants also offer advice on affordability of purchases and services.

Tax accountants prepare tax returns and must be extremely knowledgeable about federal, state, and local tax laws. For this reason, many tax accountants have prior experience in public or government accounting. Senior accountants are responsible for seeing that the organization conforms to all tax laws.

Cost accountants determine the cost of goods and services. Their work is needed by manufacturing and service industries alike. They are instrumental in determining prices that are high enough to ensure a profit but low enough to interest consumers. Cost accountants work with marketing and manufacturing staffs, and some familiarity with the work of these departments is helpful.

Internal auditing is a specialized area of management accounting that has attracted a great deal of interest in recent years. Because of the growing body of federal legislation concerning business accounting standards and public access to information about corporate finances, internal auditing has changed from the luxury it once was to an absolute necessity. The internal auditor conducts an independent appraisal from within the organization by analyzing, criticizing, and recommending improvements to internal financial practices. The internal auditor also ensures the safety and profitability of investments and assets, and seeks to uncover sources of waste and inefficiency. By virtue of being inside the organization, the internal auditor is privy to confidential information that is not shared with auditing public accountants.

In addition to being a skilled accountant, the internal auditor must have a comprehensive understanding of all fundamental business areas: marketing, manufacturing, advertising, and stockholder relations. Internal auditing is an excellent path to an executive position because of the background provided by this exposure. However, despite the thrill of investigation, internal auditing is largely a job of long hours and repetitive work; one must be an individual of exceptional diligence and concentration.

The management accounting end of the industry is aware of the need to demonstrate a commitment to high professional standards. Certification is now available to management accountants: the certificate in management accounting (C.M.A.) and the certified internal auditor (C.I.A.). The C.M.A. exam is sponsored by the National Association of Accountants and tests decision-making capability and knowledge of business law, finance, and organization. The C.I.A. exam is sponsored by the Institute of Internal Auditors and tests the theory and practice of internal auditing. Both exams are open to graduating seniors, but work experience is required for certification. Multiple certification is permissible and encouraged.

Your first assignment will depend on the size of the accounting staff and the arrangement of the department. In general accounting, for instance, you might be assigned to a specialized function, such as accounts payable. In tax accounting, you might be assigned to local, state, or federal taxes. You will probably be rotated or given some exposure to all the department functions before settling in one area. Your work will be supervised by a senior accountant.

Qualifications

Personal: Reliability. Ability to work independently. Flexibility. Discipline.

Professional: Understanding of business and the marketplace. Willingness to increase your knowledge of practical accounting techniques.

Career Paths

LEVEL	JOB TITLE	EXPERIENCE NEEDED
Entry	Junior accountant	College degree
2	Senior accountant	3-4 years
3	General accountant, department manager or chief internal auditor	4-8 years
4	Treasurer, controller, chief financial officer	15+ years

Job Responsibilities

Entry Level

THE BASICS: Bookkeeping. Writing and recording checks. Filling out tax returns. Keeping files.

MORE CHALLENGING DUTIES: Offering your ideas on improved accounting procedures. Helping to prepare reports on company finances. Learning about the accounting department's relationship with other sections of the organization.

Moving Up

From the beginning, you must demonstrate your understanding of basic accounting techniques and your ability to handle the various assignments given to you. You must master the various functions handled by your department and understand that department's place within the organization's accounting structure. Senior accountants oversee the work of junior accountants. Here your responsibilities include preparing reports and analyses of your work. More experienced accountants handle any large or unusual transactions and are responsible for financial planning. As a manager, you must start thinking in terms of the entire organization, not just the needs of the accounting department. Good business sense is the key to success, because you are no longer only an accountant; you assume wider managerial and financial responsibilities.

The controller is the executive in charge of all accounting functions and summarizes financial information for executive personnel. This individual must have a keen understanding of all business operations and the judgment to make financial planning decisions. The treasurer handles the cash flow and all financial reserves and is involved with loans, credit, and investments. Many firms combine the functions of controller and treasurer into one position.

The chief financial officer oversees the controller, treasurer, chief internal auditor, and the accounting staffs. He or she advises top executives as to the financial needs and stability of the organization. The chief financial officer does not have to be an accountant, but often this individual has accounting experience. That top financial management can rise from the ranks of accountants demonstrates the importance of the accounting department in overall policymaking.

GOVERNMENT ACCOUNTING

Government accounting attracts those graduates and experienced accountants who want to use the skills of management accounting in a different setting. Government agencies tend to pay less than private industry, but as an employer, government offers distinct advantages: job security, excellent benefits, and some unique opportunities. The goal of the accounting department of a typical government agency is to function within the budgetary constraints mandated by legislative action.

As a recent graduate, you begin as the equivalent of a junior accountant and progress with experience to management levels. The policy of most government bodies is to promote from within, so unless you have an advanced degree or specialized experience, a career in government accounting should begin soon after graduation.

The IRS is the single largest employer of accountants in the United States. The IRS particularly needs accounting graduates to be agents—the people on the receiving end of federal tax returns. This job requires strong accounting abilities and the temperament to work with taxpayers.

IRS work requires extensive entry-level training. You begin with an orientation and seven weeks of classroom training covering all aspects of tax law, fraud examination, and research techniques. Then, under the guidance of professionals, you continue your training on the job by reviewing simple taxpayer returns. Next, you receive classroom training on the examination of corporate tax returns and work with such returns. Finally, you are instructed in handling the more complex corporate returns, learning about tax shelters and other intricacies of tax law.

As you progress, you might remain a tax generalist, specialize in the returns of a particular industry, or be called on to instruct new trainees. Investigations or special projects might also require your participation.

The Securities and Exchange Commission (SEC) offers excellent opportunities for experienced C.P.A.s who have at least three years of experience working with publicly held corporations in a public accounting firm. The SEC regulates all firms that sell stock by developing general accounting and auditing regulations and reviewing such companies' compliance with these regulations. After analyzing an audit of a particular corporation, the SEC may call for an investigation.

The army has centralized its accounting staff at the United States Army Finance Accounting Center, located at Fort Benjamin Harrison in Indianapolis, IN. Job openings exist for both operations accountants, who handle daily accounting needs, and systems accountants, who develop computer-based accounting systems for military bases and offices. Once you are employed by the federal government, you can transfer to other departments and agencies. You may move to a similar position, or to one with greater responsibilities. Current employees ("status employees," as they are called) receive preference in all hiring decisions.

Opportunities at state and local levels vary, but the greatest need for accountants is normally found in the larger departments and agencies, such as those handling transportation and road maintenance, law enforcement, and tax collection.

ADDITONAL INFORMATION

Salaries

Salaries vary according to the employer's size. The following ranges for starting annual salaries are taken from Robert Haft International's 1984 study.

PUBLIC ACCOUNTING
Entry $16,500 to $19,000 (medium-size firm)
      $18,000 to $20,000 (large firm)
1-3 years' experience $18,000 to $23,000 (medium)
      $20,000 to $24,500 (large)
Senior $23,000 to $32,000 (medium) $24,000 to $34,000 (large)
Manager: $33,000 to $46,000 (medium)
      $36,000 to $56,000 (large)
Salaries are higher for C.P.A.s and those with graduate degrees.

MANAGEMENT ACCOUNTING

Entry	$15,000 to $17,000 (medium-size firm); $15,000 to $18,000 (large firm)
1-3 years' experience	$23,000 to $28,500 (medium); $18,000 to $26,000 (large)
Senior	$23,000 to $28,000 (medium); $27,000 to $31,000 (large)
Manager	$29,000 to $34,000 (medium); $33,000 to $50,000 (large)

Salaries are higher for C.P.As, those with graduate degrees, and accountants whose jobs require extensive travel.

GOVERNMENT ACCOUNTING

Government accountants are paid according to standard pay scales. For federal salaries, consult the Office of Personnel Management for current figures.

Working Conditions

Hours: Accounting is a nine-to-five job, except during tax season. The workload during this period—roughly December to May—is especially heavy for public accountants and tax accountants. Expect long hours, weekend work, and no time off.

Environment: Accounting is an office job, but surroundings vary from employer to employer. At the entry level you might share an office, have a desk in a general work area, or, at large businesses and public accounting firms, enjoy the luxury of a private office from the beginning. As you progress, your surroundings become more comfortable. Management accountants work in the administrative offices of their organizations. As an accountant for the Department of Defense, you might work as a civilian on a military base.

Workstyle: Most work is done at your desk, but public accountants frequently work at clients' offices. Management and government accountants generally have fewer opportunities to work out of the office.

Travel: Travel opportunities exist for many accounting professionals. Even in small public accounting firms, overnight travel may be required for visits to clients. In large firms, such as those of the Big Eight, you might spend days or weeks away on a single project. In management accounting, internal auditing staffers are most likely to travel; in multinational corporations this can mean international travel for experienced personnel. Certain federal departments, such as the Department of Defense, require extensive national and international travel.

Extracurricular Activities/Work Experience

Beta Alpha Psi—accounting fraternity

Alpha Kappa Psi—business administration fraternity

Treasurer or financial officer of campus organizations

Resident adviser

Internships

Many public accounting firms and businesses are willing to take interns. Investigate such possibilities on your own or through your campus internship office. Larger firms may have strict academic requirements for interns; these competitive programs are often paid internships.

Recommended Reading

BOOKS

The Big Eight by Mark Stevens, Macmillan Publishing Company: 1981

How to Speak Accounting: A Glossary of Terms with Guidance on How to Read an Annual Report by Sidney Davidson and Clyde P. Stickney, Harcourt Brace Jovanovich: 1983

The Modern Accountant's Handbook, edited by James D. Edwards and Homer A. Black, Dow-Jones-Irwin: 1976

PERIODICALS

CPA Journal (monthly), New York Society of Certified Public Accountants, 600 Third Avenue, New York, NY 10016

Government Accountants Journal (quarterly), Association of Government Accountants, 727 South 23rd Street, Arlington, VA 22202

Journal of Accountancy (monthly), American Institute of Certified Public Accountants, 1211 Avenue of the Americas, New York, NY 10036

Management Accounting (monthly), National Association of Accountants, 919 Third Avenue, New York, NY 10022

The Practical Accountant (monthly), Warren, Gorham, and Lamont, Inc., 210 South Street, Boston, MA 02111

The Wall Street Journal (daily), 23 Cortlandt Street, New York, NY 10007

Professional Associations

American Institute of Certified Public Accountants
1211 Avenue of the Americas
New York, NY 10036

American Society of Women Accountants
35 East Wacker Drive
Chicago, IL 60601

Association of Government Accountants
727 South 23rd Street
Arlington, VA 22202

Institute of Internal Auditors
249 Maitland Avenue
Altamonte Springs, FL 32701

National Association of Accountants
919 Third Avenue
New York, NY 10022

INTERVIEW

Richard Lemieux, Age 34
Manager
Ernst & Whinney, Cleveland, OH

The business environment has always fascinated me—even in high school I kept abreast of the stock market—so naturally I studied business administration in college. I was interested in a career that would be different from the usual nine-to-five routine—a profession that would provide challenge and opportunity. An internship with a Big Eight firm convinced me that public accounting was a profession I would enjoy.

The combination of a master's degree (M.B.A.) and the internship experience gave me an advantage in the job market. I started with Ernst and Whinney at a step above the entry-level position because of these qualifications, and shortly thereafter I obtained my C.P.A. certificate. The public accounting environment has more than met my requirements for a rewarding career. I work in a flexible environment; the hours are not rigid, unlike some other professions. I like the variety of engagements and special projects, and I particularly enjoy working with our clients. After ten years with Ernst & Whinney, I can honestly say I enjoy every new day.

Careers in public accounting present challenges that are not always associated with accounting. For example, many of our staff people are now working with microcomputers in order to explore their applications to the audit environment. The requirements for tax research seem to increase daily, and in the consulting area our people are involved with feasibility studies, cash flow projections, and financial forecasting.

At the present time, I am serving a tour of duty through Ernst & Whinney's national office in Cleveland, OH. This opportunity allowed me to transfer from our Portland, ME, office to work in an environment that is very different from anything I thought I'd be doing. I am now involved in a nonclient capacity, meaning that my job is part of the internal functions of our national office. Specifically, I am serving as a manager in the national personnel group, dealing mostly with the administration of personnel policy, corporate relocation, recruiting, and personnel information systems. I am also directly involved with the Ernst & Whinney Foundation, which is responsible for our firm's matching gift program as well as other grants and endowments to colleges and universities. I thoroughly enjoy this opportunity to work in the national office, but must admit that I miss having direct contact with our clients. After my tour of duty is over, I will return to one of our practice offices to continue working as a C.P.A. in the accounting and auditing environment.

BANKING

IMAGINE yourself the manager of an operations department, responsible for the global transfer of currencies worth several million dollars. Or a member of the international department, traveling to the Middle East, Africa, or Europe to check on overseas branches. Or managing a loan portfolio for a major multinational corporation, providing its chief financial officer with up-to-date financial information. Banking has become the central nervous system of the world's economy, and today's dynamic banker can be found in front of a desk-top terminal calling up the vast amount of financial data needed to provide an increasing array of new products and services. Today customers want banks to provide more than brokerage services and electronic funds transfers. If you want to be involved in a state-of-the-art business, if you have an entrepreneurial spirit, and, above all, if you are endowed with keen creativity, a career in banking is for you.

The changes in banking are primarily due to the impact of technology. Banking is now a worldwide, 24-hour-a-day business. Automated teller machines, home banking via microcomputers, and office automation have affected every bank employee. But you don't have to be a whiz kid who talks in bits and bytes to get your foot in the door. Every major bank has either a formal training program or professional on-the-job training that includes instruction in the use of the technology. What is most important is your ability to grasp the concept and quickly master the skill.

Banks recruit graduates from a wide variety of majors. In fact, half of all college students entering banking come from a liberal arts background. But don't overlook the traditional financial core courses: business, accounting, marketing, and finance. They will add to your desirability as a job candidate, as will a knowledge of computer science, production management (operations), and interpersonal communications. When a recruiter is having a hard time deciding, it is your interpersonal skills that will count most heavily.

Most banks put their college recruits through a formal training program in which they are taught the methods and practices of the particular institution. Regardless of academic background, all newcomers go into the same melting pot. Students who have taken the financial core courses mentioned will, of course, be more familiar with those subjects during the training program. However, strong analytical skills will enable you to interpret a financial statement, and here an English major who knows how to extract meaning from a careful reading of literature or a history major who knows how to spot a trend or movement in a group of facts will not be at a disadvantage to a finance major.

More and more students entering the field have had the foresight to make themselves knowledgeable about telecommunications to gain an understanding of the newly diverse world of banking. These students have a better chance of getting a job offer than those with a limited, traditional view of the industry.

Many different functional areas exist within banking, and most banks will ask you for which area you prefer to be considered. Commercial and retail banking have recruitment programs in the following functional areas:

- **Credit Lending**
- **Operations**

- **Systems**
- **Trusts**

Job Outlook

Job Openings Will Grow: Faster than average

Competition for Jobs: Keen
Expect the most competition for positions in credit lending. Expanding opportunities can be found in the operations and systems areas. As new sources for loans become harder to find, operations is being looked to for development of nonfee-based services, such as letters of credit and money transfer services. In systems, the computerization and communications systems needed to deliver customer services are implemented.

New Job Opportunities: Because of industry deregulation, banks are now actively seeking people to work in such diverse areas as mergers and acquisitions; private banking, which serves individuals with high net worth and high incomes; office automation, which develops executive information systems and implements them throughout the bank; product management, which includes the planning, pricing, and marketing of new products and services; and telecommunications, which develops the global communications channels necessary for getting and submitting information.

Geographic Job Index

Although banks can be found in any city or town, the major money centers are located in New York, NY, Chicago, IL, San Francisco, CA and Boston, MA. Opportunities at the regional or local end of the industry are growing in Dallas, TX, Houston, TX, and other cities in the Southwest.

Who the Employers Are

COMMERCIAL BANKS (or money-center banks) market their products and services to multinational corporations; to smaller banks, called correspondents; and to individuals, who use checking and loan services.

REGIONAL BANKS provide many of the same services as the larger money-center banks, but on a smaller scale. Their clients are typically locally based small and medium-size businesses.

SAVINGS AND LOAN ASSOCIATIONS offer their customers personal savings accounts and mortgages. However, under new banking legislation, they are allowed to make commercial and business loans.

Major Employers

COMMERCIAL BANKS
>Bank of America, San Francisco, CA
>Bankers Trust Company, New York, NY
>Chase Manhattan Bank, New York, NY
>Chemical Bank, New York, NY
>Citibank, New York, NY
>Continental Illinois National Bank, Chicago, IL
>First National Bank of Boston, Boston, MA
>First National Bank of Chicago, Chicago, IL
>Manufacturers Hanover Trust Company, New York, NY
>Security Pacific National Bank, Los Angeles, CA

REGIONAL BANKS
>First Bank System, Minneapolis, MN
>Mellon Bank, Pittsburgh, PA
>Mercantile Bank, St. Louis, MO
>NCNB National Bank, Charlotte, NC
>Ranier National Bank, Seattle, WA
>Republic Bank Dallas, Dallas, TX
>Wachovia Bank & Trust Company, Winston-Salem, NC

How to Break into the Field

Most banks have formal on-campus recruitment programs through which they hire most of their trainees. They frequently recruit separately for each major functional area: credit lending, operations, systems, and trusts. Be sure to check schedules carefully to ensure an appointment in your area of interest.

Before the interview, do your homework. Learn all you can about the internal workings of the area for which you plan to interview. If your field of interest is not represented, select the next most appropriate area and ask the recruiter to forward your résumé to the proper section. Also, learn something about the bank itself. Different banks have different personalities. Some are aggressive, others more traditional and conservative. Try to interview with banks that have a corporate identity compatible with your own personal identity.

Landing a summer internship is another pathway to a full-time position. Most major banks have internship programs, although they are usually limited to graduate students. Recruitment for the internships is usually done through campus visits. Check with your placement office for details.

If your college does not have a formal placement office, or if the bank to which you wish to apply is not recruiting on your campus, send a well-written letter, accompanied by a résumé, to the bank's director of college recruitment. Follow up your letter with a phone call.

Whether you have an on-campus interview or are writing directly to the college recruitment department, never pass up help from anyone who knows someone at the bank. A well-placed word can be invaluable.

International Job Opportunities

At a large commercial bank, and even at some regional banks, overseas work is possible. International department lending officers may be assigned to work abroad for a period of three to five years, or may be required to travel abroad frequently. Corporate department staffs that handle U.S. multinational corporations also do quite a bit of business overseas.

Most banks try to staff their overseas branches with local citizens. Only the higher-level managerial jobs may be filled by Americans. Specialized positions in areas such as investment banking, joint ventures, and trade go to M.B.A.s or other experienced personnel. Fluency in a foreign language is helpful but not essential, because most banks have contracts with language schools to provide training as necessary.

CREDIT LENDING

This is the most visible area of banking, the area that involves the traditional bank-client relationship that almost everyone associates with the industry. However, this aspect of banking is more than just extending credit or offering interest-bearing accounts to clients. In consumer banking, a lending officer assesses the creditworthiness of individuals. In commercial banking, a lending officer evaluates the financial status of corporations or nonprofit organizations; performs industry surveys, analyzing a particular industry to determine if backing a firm in that area is a good loan risk; makes production forecasts to see if a borrowing firm's available resources will meet production requirements; predicts how a loan would affect the bank's cash flow positively or negatively; or handles corporate overdrafts, contacting corporate customers whose payments are late.

To start out you will go on customer calls with experienced loan officers and be responsible for taking notes and writing a report on the customer and the loan review—not as a participant, but as an observer. You may be called on to research new business prospects, making cold calls to prospects in a given territory or industry. At a smaller bank, your responsibilities will be broader and you will actually make decisions on modest loans quite early.

Qualifications

Personal: Strong analytical skills. Ability to conceptualize. An affinity for quantitative problems. Strong negotiation skills. Extremely good interpersonal skills.

Professional: Ability to analyze data and financial statements and do creative financial planning. Familiarity with bank products and services. Ability to present clearly written reports.

Career Paths

LEVEL	JOB TITLE	EXPERIENCE NEEDED
Entry	Trainee	College degree
2	Assistant Loan Officer	1-2 years
3	Loan Officer/Branch manager	3-5 years
4	Loan manager	7+ years

Job Responsibilities

Entry Level

THE BASICS: Training will consist of both classroom instruction in such areas as finance, accounting, and credit analysis, and actual account work, helping lending officers make judgments about existing or potential bank relationships.

MORE CHALLENGING DUTIES: Upon completion of training, you will be assigned to a line lending area, attend advanced banking seminars, and have the opportunity to meet with customers.

Moving Up

Your advancement will depend on your ability to establish advantageous client relationships, to close lucrative loan deals successfully, and to know when not to approve a loan. As you advance, the loan review process will become more complex and involve significantly more money. You can measure your success by your approval authority—how big a loan you are authorized to approve without going to a higher level of management.

OPERATIONS

The most successful banks anticipate and satisfy all their customers' financial needs. Operations occupies a front-row seat in the banking industry because it has bankwide responsibility for providing customers with nonfee-based (nonloan) services—letters of credit, money transfers, and foreign exchange—services of increased importance because banks can no longer make the profits they once did by lending money to customers. The operations department is usually the largest department of a commercial bank. The Chase Manhattan Bank operations department, for example, has more than 4,000 employees. Graduates are employed in supervisory positions, managing the clerical staff, with responsibility for setting up assignments and time schedules, evaluating performance, making sure work is done properly, training new employees, and authorizing salary increases. Work in operations also involves troubleshooting for customers, solving their account problems, for example, by tracing a money transfer that was never credited.

Qualifications

Personal: Ability to meet deadlines. Ability to perform under pressure. Ability to get along with many different types of people.

Professional: Ability to understand and follow through on complex instructions. Familiarity with concepts or computer science or a related discipline. Knowledge of fee-based services and products.

Career Paths

LEVEL	JOB TITLE	EXPERIENCE NEEDED
Entry	Operations Trainee	College degree
2	Supervisor	18 months
3	Department manager	3-5 years
4	Division manager	6+ years

Job Responsibilities

Entry Level

THE BASICS: You begin your career in operations either in a formal training program, or, more likely, on the job. You will be an operations trainee for about 18 months, learning by rotating among the various departments that handle fee-based services.

MORE CHALLENGING DUTIES: After the training period, you will be assigned to a department or a staff area such as financial management or budget coordination and will learn about a single product or area in depth.

Moving Up

Your progress will depend on your ability to improve the overall productivity of your department or area, to motivate your staff, to stay within your budget, and to complete transactions efficiently and accurately. Because operations is not exclusively devoted to production management, for further advancement you will need to learn about product development, marketing, and systems functions. Those who move into these areas often accompany loan officers on customer calls, offering the technical advice that will help clinch a deal or presenting a plan to customize an existing product to meet the client's expanding needs.

With hard work and diligence you can acquire the knowledge and expertise that will enable you to move almost anywhere in the bank organization. Operations managers can move into marketing positions, the systems areas, or perhaps relocate (even overseas) to manage a branch bank.

SYSTEMS

The systems area is now involved in every banking decision from credit lending to recruitment. Most large commercial banks have both a central systems area and separate decentralized systems units that service the major components of the organization. Systems is responsible for developing, implementing, and maintaining automated programs for clients and for in-house use; for selecting hardware, writing software, and consulting with the user-client when special programs must be developed. In addition, systems staffers must keep up with the latest developments in technological applications and services.

Qualifications

Personal: Ability to think in analytical terms. Ease in working with abstract models.

Professional: Quantitative skills. Familiarity with the business applications of software and hardware. Ability to convert technical language and concepts into familiar and understandable terms.

Career Paths

LEVEL	JOB TITLE	EXPERIENCE NEEDED
Entry	Systems trainee	College degree
2	Systems analyst	2 years
3	Systems consultant	3 years
4	Senior systems consultant	5 years

Job Responsibilities

Entry Level

THE BASICS: Either in a structured training program or through on-the-job-training, you will become familiar with the bank's hardware and software and how they are used. Depending on your background, you may become a programmer, or you may be placed on a systems team project, refining the use of current equipment or developing systems for as yet unmet needs.

MORE CHALLENGING DUTIES: Applying your skills to more difficult or specialized projects.

Moving Up

If you demonstrate interpersonal skills as well as technical ability, you could become a project manager, overseeing a team of systems people working on the development and implementation of a specific systems capability, such as a new internal telephone switching system or software for an executive work station, which could include features such as electronic mail and word processing.

The potential for a talented systems person is excellent. You could end up managing an operations or office automation department, developing and installing new systems, or becoming a systems consultant for overseas branches. Successful systems personnel can move into any department in the bank.

TRUSTS

The trust department manages and invests money, property, or other assets owned by a client. The pension plans of large corporations and other organizations often use trusts, as do individuals with large assets. Many estates are also managed in trust by the provisions of a will. Like the credit department, this department deals closely and extensively with clients. The training program is similar to that in other areas of banking, but in general advancement is slower and requires more experience.

Qualifications

Personal: A straightforward manner. Accuracy. Good with numbers. Patience in dealing with people. Confidence.

Professional: Strong analytical ability. Good business judgment. Ability to apply financial theory to practical problems.

Career Paths

LEVEL	JOB TITLE	EXPERIENCE NEEDED
Entry	Trainee	College degree
2	Assistant trust officer	1-3 years
3	Trust officer	4-6 years
4	Senior trust officer	10+ years

Job Responsibilities

Entry Level

THE BASICS: Developing familiarity with bank policies and procedures.

MORE CHALLENGING POSITIONS: Researching investments, real estate, or the overall economy to assist superiors. Some contact with clients.

Moving Up

Showing sound judgment and an ability to work independently will garner an assignment to manage some of the smaller trust funds. Moving up also depends on your ability to attract new customers to the bank, as well as to keep present clients satisfied. As you advance you will become responsible for handling more and more money. Top-level trust officers are expected not only to bring in substantial new business and to handle the largest accounts, but also to manage and support lower-level employees.

ADDITIONAL INFORMATION

Salaries

Salaries vary according to the size of the bank. The following figures are taken from Robert Half International's 1984 survey:

Installment loans/assistant manager: $18,000 to $22,000 (small bank); $21,000 to $27,000 (medium-size bank); $23,500 to $28,500 (large bank).

Commercial loans/branch manager: $22,000 to $28,000 (small); $24,000 to $31,000 (medium); $26,000 to $31,000 (large).

Senior loan officer: $28,000 to $32,000 (small); $33,000 to $37,000 (medium); $33,000 to $50,000 (large).

Mortgage loans: $23,500 to $32,000 (small); $28,000 to $36,000 (medium); $32,000 to $41,000 (large).

Operations officer: $17,000 to $21,000 (small); $22,000 to $29,000 (medium); $24,000 to $31,000 (large).

Trust officer: $22,000 to $29,500 (small); $23,000 to $30,000 (medium); $27,500 to $40,000 (large).

Working Conditions

Hours: The credit trainee rarely sees daylight, because long hours and weekend work are often required to get through the training program. After training, normal hours will be whatever it takes to get the job done (nine to five plus). The hours in operations are different because it is a 24-hour-a-day shop. Night shifts and weekend work may be unavoidable, especially for less experienced employees. Systems staffers may also work on a 24-hour clock; the hours are longest when new systems are being installed and deadlines must be met.

Environment: Lending officers get the choicest locations in the bank; because their job is customer-oriented, the surroundings are usually plush and pleasant. The operations and systems departments take a 360-degree turn from the lending department; the workspace is strictly functional, with few amenities.

Workstyle: In credit, much time is spent researching facts and figures about existing and prospective clients, which could take you from the bank library to the client's headquarters. The rest of your time will largely be spent in conference with senior lending officers. Operations and systems work is desk work. Managers walk the area, talking with the staff and lending assistance. In both departments, senior people may meet occasionally with systems consultants.

Travel: Travel is rare for entry-level employees in any bank. Later, however, lending officers in consumer banking might travel throughout their state. In commercial banking, research could take a lending officer to major cities throughout the country. If you are assigned to the international department in credit, operations, or systems, you might be sent to overseas branches.

Extracurricular Activities/Work Experience

Experience as a cashier/teller

Clerical experience

Financial officer/treasurer in campus organizations

Internships

Many banks—savings and loan associations and consumer and commercial banks—are willing to take interns, especially in summer programs. Interns are paid, and the experience may result in a job offer after graduation. Your campus placement office is the best source of information regarding these programs. If your school does not have a placement office, contact the college recruitment director at banks that interest you for details.

Recommended Reading

BOOKS

All You Need to Know About Banks by John Cook and Robert Wood, Bantam Books: 1983

The Bankers by Martin Mayer, Ballantine Books: 1980

In Banks We Trust by Penny Lernoux, Doubleday & Company: 1984

Money: Bank of the Eighties by Dimitris Chorafas, Petrocelli: 1981

Money and Banking by Richard W. Lindholm, Littlefield, Adams & Company: 1969

The New Age of Banking by George Sterne, Profit Ideas: 1981

Polk's World Bank Directory, R. L. Polk and Company (semiannual directory listing banks by city, state, and foreign country)

Your Career in Banking, American Bankers Association: 1980

PERIODICALS

ABA Banking Journal (monthly), 345 Hudson Street, New York, NY 10014

American Banker (daily), One State Street Plaza, New York, NY 10004

The Banker's Magazine (bimonthly), Warren, Gorham, and Lamont, Inc., 210 South Street, Boston, MA 02111

Bank News (monthly), 912 Baltimore Avenue, Kansas City, MO 64105

Professional Associations

American Bankers Association
1120 Connecticut Avenue, N.W.
Washington, DC 20036

Consumer Bankers Association
1725 K Street, N.W.
Washington, DC 20006

National Association of Bank Women
111 East Wacker Drive
Chicago, IL 60601

United States League of Savings Associations
111 East Wacker Drive
Chicago, IL 60601

INTERVIEWS

Louise D'Imperio, Age 22
Operations Analyst
Chase Manhattan Bank, New York, NY

My association with Chase began while I was a student at Villanova University. During summer breaks, I was a member of the apprenticeship management training program, which places undergraduates in operations. The program provides quality relief for full-time employees who take vacations.

I worked in the interbank compensation department, which is responsible for the settlement of funds transfer errors. I worked in the staff support section, which supports the production line. I began by doing simple clerical functions, but later became involved in numbers crunching for production tracking reports. In my final summer, I was an inquiry clerk. My responsibility was to take customer and other bank questions over the phone and via telex and inform the individual of the outcome of the compensation case or reconcile any errors made in settling the case.

In that department I started from the ground up. After three summers, I really knew how a case was initiated and processed, and I had a knowledge of the problems that can arise. But after I graduated in May 1983 I wanted a job outside of bank operations. I have a B.S. in business administration with a concentration in marketing. I wanted a marketing-oriented job and I wanted to be involved in product positioning.

Because I had contacts at Chase, I was able to bypass the normal channels that graduates go through. I looked outside of banking, and mailed résumés to various departments at Chase. Among others, I got a response from Chase international operations and systems.

I chose the position in international operations and systems because I felt that a job in office automation would open up an interesting career path. I knew very little about the field of office automation, but was very interested in it. I work in a division that is concerned with office automation in the international section— more specifically, smaller Chase branches abroad. I'm involved in the marketing and support function of the division, which markets office automation products internally. We want to increase the productivity of individual branches, and we want to increase the use of our products. Our work involves training, consultation, and the development of customized software.

The brunt of my work is project-oriented. Right now I'm working on a project that examines what office automation may do for one of Chase's small subsidiaries. I also edit an office automation newsletter, which takes up about 40 percent of my time, and have written documentation for some of the software developed by our group.

I knew nothing about office automation when I started this job; I actually thought that it involved only word processing. Office automation goes way beyond word processing to include a variety of technologies. My background in operations was not a requirement for this job, but it has made it easier to view the workings of the bank. It also showed me how much I still have to learn about banking. I enjoy my job and I like being involved with technologies that have a definite impact on productivity.

Jayne Geisler, Age 32
Vice President, Market and Financial Planning
Chemical Bank, New York, NY

After receiving a B.A. degree in mathematics and French in 1973 from the State University College of New York at Potsdam, I entered the M.S. teaching program at Boston College, which combined coursework with a part-time teaching position in high school mathematics. Finding teaching unchallenging and realizing my abilities would be better utilized in the business environment, I entered banking, an industry where I felt I could capitalize on my quantitative background

I joined Chemical Bank in 1974 as a financial analyst in the finance, then control, division. My responsiblities included cost accounting and financial management reporting for the consumer banking and upstate regions of the metropolitan (New York) division. Specifically this consisted of preparing, analyzing, and monitoring the financial performance of these business segments against budget and prior years, plus the development of unit and product costs of various banking services. The work was entirely hands-on, with no formal training program, and provided me with a broad understanding of the mechanics of the banking industry.

In 1977 I transferred to the controller's area of the metropolitan division where my duties expanded to include perormance reporting and analysis for the commercial as well as consumer lending areas of the division, acting as a liaison with these areas, plus coordinating their annual budgets. In addition, I was charged with designing and implementing a management information system for evaluating the financial performance of these business segments against budget.

Since 1975 I had been working toward my M.B.A. in finance at night from New York University. Coming from a nonbusiness educational background, I felt that it was apparent that an M.B.A. was necessary to enhance my professional development and my future career goals. It provided me with an understanding of the interrelationships among the key business ingredients—finance, economics, marketing, management, and accounting—which I thought necessary to be more effective in my job. As a result, I am of the opinion that an M.B.A. is an excellent degree for enhancing one's background, especially for those with a liberal arts education. However, I strongly believe that business school is more meaningful and relevant to those who have had prior work experience, as there exists a context in which to augment the course of study.

Upon completion of my M.B.A. in February 1979 I entered the bank's commercial credit training program in order to be a part of the bank's basic business—lending—and to round out my banking experience. I was assigned to the district specializing in the garment/textile/entertainment industries. Handling a portfolio of small business and middle market customers was a challenge. I analyzed and determined credit needs, structured deals, and provided cash management servicing.

Late in 1980 I was asked to join the division's strategic planning unit, which was then undergoing expansion. After a little more than a year as deputy department head, I was promoted to director of the unit, which is my current position. Planning has become increasingly important due to the deregulation of the banking industry. "What do we do now? Where do we want to be in five years? What new products/services should we offer?" These are just some of the challenges facing us as we anticipate the changes in banking law and the movements of our competition. In view of this changing environment created by deregulation, I began working toward a law degree to further supplement my background and experience.

Banking is experiencing tremendous growth and change—it's a whole new ballgame—evolving into a fully integrated financial services industry. The competition not only includes banking institutions, but has expanded to comprise brokerage and investment houses, retailers, high-tech companies, conglomerates, and so forth. As a result, those individuals seeking to enter the industry

will need to be sales-oriented and well-rounded in financial services. Banking, finance, and credit will provide the basis, but
securities, insurance, and other financial services will play key
parts in the banking financial supermarket.

DEPARTMENT STORE RETAILING

CONSUMERS generally take for granted that they will always find their favorite department stores brimming with merchandise. Unnoticed by most customers, a large, talented staff works long, hard hours to keep the shelves filled, the selection varied, the stores beautiful, and the business of retailing running smoothly. Retailing is an industry in which brains and diligence can take you to high levels of decision-making years before your contemporaries in other fields have reached similar positions of responsibility.

Graduates of virtually any discipline may enter department store retailing. Prospective employers are looking for demonstrated capacity to learn and make quick, sound judgments and are less interested in academic backgrounds. You must be flexible, comfortable with people, self-disciplined, and highly motivated—and a sense of humor certainly does not hurt. Retailing is a high-pressure profession where no slow seasons exist—only busy and busier, with the November-December pre-Christmas rush being the most hectic time of all. Prior retail experience, even a summer spent behind a cash register, is a plus; some retailers won't consider candidates without it.

Most entry-level jobs are in merchandising, an area further divided into:

- **Store Management**
- **Buying**

Your job in merchandising begins with a training period of six months to a year. Some trainees divide their time between classroom learning and work experience, others train entirely on the job. Generally, the larger the retailer, the more formalized the training. Whether you enter the field via store management or buying depends primarily on the employer. Many stores separate these functions beginning at the entry level; you must choose which path you prefer. Other stores will introduce all new merchandising personnel to buying and later allow those interested in and qualified for management to move up. The opposite arrangement, moving into buying at some later stage, also occurs, although infrequently.

The modern store is reaping the benefits of the technological revolution. Point-of-sale computer terminals are replacing mechanical cash registers; these automatically compute sales, taxes, and discounts and simplify inventory control by keeping sales records. Computers are also used for credit records and tracking sales forecasts.

Retailing is vulnerable to downturns in the economy, but it's one of the first industries to bounce back after a recession. As a highly profit-oriented business, it's hectic and competitive. The customer's satisfaction and loyalty to the store are very important, which means that you must tolerate and even pamper people whom you may not like. In retailing, the unexpected is the order of the day; you can expect to feel pressured, but seldom unchallenged.

Job Outlook

Job Openings Will Grow: As fast as average

Competition for Jobs: Keen

In merchandising, the most competition exists in buying; this area has fewer openings, tends to pay a bit better, and has an aura of glamour about it.

New Job Opportunities: An exciting new technological development, still in experimental form, that may change retailing in the next decade is video retailing. A select number of communities now have a two-way cable television system through which viewers may receive and send information to a broadcasting center. Viewers can order goods seen on the screen by typing their selections on a keyboard. Video retailing is still in developmental form, but those entering retailing should be aware of its potential as a new job area.

Geographic Job Index

The location of retail jobs parallels the distribution of the general population; stores operate where customers live. As an up-and-coming executive in a retail chain, expect to work in a city or suburban area. Most new store construction in the coming years is expected to take place in revitalizing city cores. Department stores are found across the country, with the highest concentration of jobs in the Northeast, Midwest and West Coast.

If your interest is buying, your geographic options are more limited. For many department store chains, most or all buying takes place in a few key markets, notably New York, NY.

Who the Employers Are

A retailer is, in its simplest definition, a third party who sells a producer's goods to a consumer for a profit. The retailing industry as a whole comprises a wide variety of stores of different sizes with different personnel needs. Management personnel are sought by all major retail firms, including grocery, drug, specialty, and variety store chains, but because the most varied opportunities are found in department stores, this chapter focuses on this sector of retailing.

Major Employers

Allied Stores Corporation, New York, NY
  Bonwit Teller
  Field's
  Jordan Marsh
  Stern's

Carter Hawley Hale Stores, Los Angeles, CA
  Bergdorf Goodman
  The Broadway
  John Wanamaker
  Neiman-Marcus

Dayton Hudson Corporation, Minneapolis, MN
  Dayton's
  Diamond's

Federated Department Stores, New York, NY
  Abraham & Straus
  Bullock's
  Filene's
  Foley's
  I. Magnin
  Rich's

R.H. Macy & Company, New York, NY

Montgomery Ward & Company, Chicago, IL

J. C. Penney Company, New York, NY

Sears, Roebuck & Company, Chicago, IL

How to Break into the Field

Your best bet is on-campus interviews. Major retailers actively recruit on college campuses. This is the most accessible way to most potential employers. Don't hesitate, however, to contact employers directly, especially if you want to work for a smaller operation. Read the business section of your newspaper regularly to find out about store expansions, the addition of new stores or locations, and other developments in retailing that can provide important clues to new job openings. Keep in mind that retail or selling experience of any kind will increase your chances of getting hired.

International Job Opportunities

Extremely limited. Opportunities to live abroad exist at the corporate level of a few international chains.

STORE MANAGEMENT

If you're a "people person," consider the store management side of merchandising. You'll be responsible for handling the needs of staff and customers.

The job of store management personnel, even at entry level, entails making decisions on your own. But since decisions often have to be made on the spot and involve balancing the interests of both customers and the store, your mistakes are likely to be highly visible. Whether you manage the smallest department or a very large store, you must always keep the bottom line—making a profit—in mind when making decisions.

During training, you will work with experienced managers and will be moved throughout the store to observe all aspects of merchandising. If you're quick to learn and demonstrate management potential, you'll soon be made manager of a small department or assistant manager of a large one. You will have a fair amount of autonomy, but you must stick to store standards and implement policies determined by higher level management.

Qualifications

Personal: Ability to learn quickly. Enormous enthusiasm. The flexibility to handle a constantly changing schedule. Willingness to work weekends, holidays, and nights.

Professional: Demonstrated leadership ability. Ability to work with figures, finances, inventories, and quotas. A sense of diplomacy.

Career Paths

LEVEL	JOB TITLE	EXPERIENCE NEEDED
Entry	Department manager trainee	College degree
2	Group department manager	2-3 years
3	Assistant store manager	5-10 years
4	Store manager	8-12 years

Job Responsibilities

Entry Level

THE BASICS: Handling staff scheduling. Dealing with customer complaints. Doing plenty of paperwork.

MORE CHALLENGING DUTIES: Monitoring and motivating your sales staff. Assisting in the selection of merchandise for your department. Making decisions and solving problems.

Moving Up

Advancement in store management depends on how well you shoulder responsibility and take advantage of opportunities to learn. Effectively leading your staff, moving merchandise, and, above all, turning a profit will secure your promotion into higher levels.

Your first management position will be overseeing a small department, handling greater volumes of money and merchandise. The group department manager directs several department managers, coordinating store operations on a larger scale. From here you might progress to assistant store manager and store manager; this last position is, in many respects, similar to running a private business. The best may then go on to the corporate level.

Relocation is often necessary in order to win promotions. Switching store locations every three years or so is not uncommon. However, depending on the chain, a change of workplace need not require a change of address; often stores are within easy driving distance of each other. But the larger the chain, the greater the possibility that you'll have to move to a different city to further your career.

BUYING

Do you fantasize about a shopping spree in the world's fashion capitals? A few lucky buyers, after years of work and experience, are paid to do just that when they're sent to Hong Kong, Paris, or Milan to select new lines of merchandise. Most do not make it to such heights, but on a smaller scale, this is the business of buying.

A buyer decides which goods will be available in a store. Buyers authorize merchandise purchases from wholesalers and set the retail prices. A sensitivity to changing trends, tastes, and styles and an ability to understand and forecast the preference of your own store's customers is crucial. Buyers must also maintain standards of quality while keeping within certain ranges of affordability.

The buyer who works for a discount department store faces a particularly tough job. Obtaining lower-than-average prices for quality merchandise is a real challenge and requires an unerring eye and an ability to negotiate with sellers.

Astute buying translates into profits for the store and advancement for your career. Learning how to spend large sums of money wisely takes practice. Fortunately, as a new buyer you can afford to make a few mistakes, even an occasional expensive one, without jeopardizing your career. A good buyer takes calculated risks, and as you gain experience more of your choices will succeed.

During training, you'll work immediately as an assistant to an experienced buyer. The trainee progresses by observing, asking questions, and offering to take on appropriate responsibilities.

Qualifications

Personal: An interest in changing trends and fashions. An ability to work with a wide variety of personalities. A willingness to channel creativity into a commercial enterprise.

Professional: Financial and negotiating know-how. Organizational skills. Good judgment in spotting trends and evaluating products.

Career Paths

LEVEL	JOB TITLE	EXPERIENCE NEEDED
Entry	Assistant or junior buyer	College degree and store training
2	Buyer (small lines)	2-5 years
3	Buyer (large lines)	4-10 years
4	Corporate merchandise manager	15+ years

Job Responsibilities

Entry Level

THE BASICS: Assisting your supervising buyer. Placing orders and speaking with manufacturers by phone. Supervising the inspection and unpacking of new merchandise and overseeing its distribution.

MORE CHALLENGING DUTIES: Becoming acquainted with various manufacturers' lines. Considering products for purchase. Evaluating your store's needs. Keeping an eye on the competition.

Moving Up

Advancement depends on proof of your ability to judge customer needs and to choose saleable goods. The only purchases closely scrutinized by higher authorities are those inconsistent with past practices and standards.

After completing your training, you will first buy for a small department, then, as you become seasoned, for larger departments. High-placed buyers make decisions in buying for a key department common to several stores, for an entire state, or possibly for many stores. Your buying plans must always be well coordinated with the needs of store management.

ADDITIONAL INFORMATION

Salaries

Entry-level salaries range from $12,000 to $18,000 a year, depending on the employer and the geographic location of the store. Junior buyers tend to be among the best paid entry-level employees.

The following salary ranges show typical annual salaries for experienced retail personnel. In merchandising salaries vary with the size and importance of your department.

2-4 years:	$16,000-24,000
5-10 years:	$22,000-27,000
12 years or more:	$25,000 and up

Working Conditions

Hours: Most retail personnel work a five-day, 40-hour week, but schedules vary with different positions. In store management, daily shifts are rarely nine to five, because stores are open as many as 12 hours a day, seven days a week. Night, weekend, and holiday duty are unavoidable, especially for newcomers. Operations personnel work similar hours. Buyers have more regular schedules and are rarely asked to work evening and weekend hours.

Environment: In merchandising, your time is divided between the office and the sales floor—more often the latter. Office space at the entry level may or may not be private, depending on the store. Whether you share space or not, expect to be close to the sales floor. Merchandising is no place for those who need absolute privacy and quiet in order to be productive.

Workstyle: In store management, office time is 100 percent work; every valuable moment must be used effectively to keep on top of the paperwork. On the floor you will be busy overseeing the arrangement of merchandise, meeting with your sales staff, and listening to customer complaints. Long hours on your feet will test your patience and endurance, but you can never let the weariness show. In buying, office time is spent with paperwork and calls to manufacturers. You might also review catalog copy and illustrations. On the sales floor, you'll meet with store personnel to see how merchandise is displayed and, most important, to see how the customers are responding. Manufacturers' representatives will visit to show their products, and you might spend some days at manufacturer and wholesaler showrooms. Because these jobs bring you into the public eye, you must be well dressed and meticulously groomed. The generous discounts that employees receive as a fringe benefit help defray the cost of maintaining a wardrobe.

Travel: In store management, your responsibility lies with your own department and your own store; travel opportunities are virtually nonexistent, except for some top-level personnel. Buyers, particularly those who live outside major manufacturing centers, may make annual trips to New York, NY, and other key cities. You might also travel to trade shows at which your type of merchandise is displayed.

Extracurricular Activities/Work Experience

Leadership in campus organizations

Treasurer or financial officer of an organization

Sales position on the yearbook or campus newspaper

Summer or part-time work in any aspect of retailing

Internships

Arrange internships with individual stores or chains; many are eager to hire interns, preferring students who are in the fall semester of their senior year. Check with your school's placement or internship office or with the store itself in the spring for a fall internship. Summer internships are also available with some stores. Contact the placement office or the personnel departments of individual stores for details.

Recommended Reading

BOOKS

Buyer's Manual, National Retail Merchants Association: 1979

Creative Selling: A Programmed Approach by R.J. Burley, Addison-Wesley: 1982

The Retail Revolution: Market Transformation, Investment, and Labor in the Modern Department Store by Barry Bluestone et al., Auburn House: 1981

The Woolworths by James Brough, McGraw-Hill: 1982

PERIODICALS

Advertising Age (weekly), Crain Communications, 740 North Rush Street, Chicago, IL 60611

Journal of Retailing (quarterly), New York University, 202 Tisch Building, New York, NY 10003

Stores (monthly), National Retail Merchants Association, 100 West 31st Street, New York, NY 10001

Women's Wear Daily (daily), Fairchild Publications, Inc., 7 East 12th Street, New York, NY 10003

Professional Associations

American Marketing Association
250 South Wacker Drive
Chicago, IL 60606

American Retail Federation
1616 H Street, N.W.
Washington, DC 20006

Association of General Merchandise Chains
1625 I Street, N.W.
Washington, DC 20006

National Retail Merchants Association
100 West 31st Street
New York, NY 10001

INTERVIEWS

Carolyn Egan, Age 33
Fashion Coordinator
Bloomingdale's Department Store, NY

My first job was far removed from retailing—I taught high school math for a year. But the school environment really didn't excite me and I felt I could get more from a job. I saw an ad for the position of fashion coordinator at a branch of Gimbels' department store. I wasn't planning a career in retailing, but because I kept up with fashion and felt I had a flair for it, I applied. I got the job and enjoyed the work, but that particular branch was not a high-caliber store, and after two years I was ready to move on.

I took a part-time job as an assistant manager at an Ann Taylor store, one of a chain selling women's clothing. At that time I was also going to school to finish an art degree. My job included store management and some limited buying. I wound up managing my own store, but because Ann Taylor has a small management staff, I felt there wasn't enough growth potential. I came to know the man who was doing store design for the chain. He was expanding his operations and needed help, so I went to work with him. I designed store interiors and fixtures, which gave me a whole new perspective on the industry. I have been lucky to see so many sides of retailing, but these job changes also required me to relocate.

When I moved into fashion coordination with Bloomingdale's about seven years ago, I finally found what I had been looking for—a high-powered, high-pressured environment. When I walk into the store each morning I feel that things are moving, happening. That's the fun of retailing.

My responsibility is to work with the buyers, helping them choose the right styles. After you've been in retailing a number of years, you know where fashion has been and you can see where it's going. You decide—really by making educated guesses—what the public will want a year from today. My job includes a lot of travel—usually eight or nine weeks a year. Where there are products abroad, we explore them. That's the only way to keep up with the competition.

In buying we speak of hundreds of dozens, so you must be volume-oriented. You ask, "What does our regular customer want to see?" Then you make a decision that has to be more right than wrong. I work with children's wear, a department that rarely sees radical changes in style. But there are always new trends in color and design, and new products.

One of the toughest parts of my job is training new buyers and helping with their first big buys. They are understandably nervous about spending several hundred thousand dollars. The fashion coordinator is one with buying experience. You offer better advice if you understand the pressure and monetary responsibility of the buyer's job.

Even though I'm in a creative area, business and financial concerns are of the highest importance. You must have a head for business in every retailing job. You want to find beautiful quality products, but if they don't sell, you've failed.

The one drawback to my job is advancement. My talents and experience are best used right where I am now. Unlike the buyers, I really have no place higher to go. But I enjoy my work. I suppose it's like being an artist, and how many artists are really appreciated?

G. G. Michelson, Age 58
Senior Vice President for External Affairs
R. H. Macy & Company, NY

My job is a rather unique one—it had never existed before and was tailored just for me. I represent the company in the community in its relationships with government, and in philanthropy. I was the senior vice president for personnel and labor relations in the New York division before moving into the corporate side about five years ago.

I was given this opportunity because of my long association and familiarity with the company and the business. We have a separate public relations department, and I don't interfere with their plans; rather, I am involved in considerations of corporate policy. For example, I handle difficult shareholder and community questions. We have a substantial philanthropy budget to work with. We want to spend this money creatively, but our charitable actions must be in line with our business decisions. We are primarily concerned with the communities in which our stores are located, because we recognize our obligation to those places in which we make our living.

I was quite young when I graduated from college, so I went on to law school to mature and get that valuable credential—but I never intended to practice law. All along I knew that I wanted to work in labor relations.

I considered manufacturing and some of the heavy industries as potential employers, and I came to realize that retailing as a service industry was far more people-intensive than other businesses. I found that in retailing the personnel function had a great deal more status and received more attention from top management. Looking elsewhere, I noticed that the emphasis was on cost control, not people development.

I went directly into Macy's training program from law school. The training program was and, of course, still is largely devoted to merchandising. I worked in merchandising only for the six months that I trained, but that experience gave me an excellent background for understanding the business and the people in it. In employee relations, I had responsibility for hiring, training, and developing our employees and merchandising talent.

In the past ten years, I have seen a significant change in the kind of graduates entering retailing. We now hire a great many graduates who once would have pursued other careers—graduates certified to teach, for instance—and people with liberal arts backgrounds who once would have gone on to grad school. We have always hired people who have broad educations; we have never been too concerned about a candidate's business background. We develop our talent by training people for top management, so we are looking for the ability to learn and grow. We don't want to have to train a person to think for the first time!

I spend a lot of time seeing and counseling young people who are investigating careers. My advice: be expansive and open to unforeseen opportunities. So many graduates have rigid plans—which I jokingly refer to as their "five-year plans." Often the best things that happen in a person's career development are totally unexpected. Bright people should be more flexible than many seem to be.

GOVERNMENT

SETTING aside any judgment on the controversy about the size of government—is it too big, or not big enough?—the simple fact is that today government is the single largest employer in the United States. Millions work for federal, state, and local governments in an endless variety of jobs. Virtually every profession and trade found in the private and nonprofit sectors are found in the public sector. Whatever your skills and interests, and whatever profession you have chosen to pursue, a place may be waiting for you in government service.

For many people, government is more than an employer, it is a career choice in itself. They find government service appealing because they know that their efforts contribute to the nation, the state, or the community. On the less idealistic side, many government jobs, particularly those at the federal level, offer excellent opportunities for on-the-job training. Often you can move quickly into a management position. Government also offers exceptional benefits and job security.

Economists are needed by various government agencies and departments to monitor the vast sums of money they spend. Economists investigate the feasibility of existing or proposed policies, projects, and programs. Those with graduate degrees have the best chance of being offered a job, but if your academic record is superior and you have some research experience, you will be considered for some entry positions with just a bachelor's degree.

Government also provides a number of other unique personal and career opportunities not found elsewhere. Three opportunities with the federal government that should be of special interest to the economics major are:

- **The Peace Corps**
- **Intelligence Services**
- **Foreign Service**

If you are intrigued by any of these, begin your investigation early in your academic career. Each is highly selective and requires specific skills and experience. You must be well prepared by the time you graduate in order to compete.

Job Outlook

Job Openings Will Grow: More slowly than average

Competition for Jobs: Keen
Government hiring policies at the local, state, and federal levels are affected by political decisions. By decree or legislative action, a new department, agency, or bureau may be created, an established organization eliminated, or existing offices merged. Since 1980, a strong movement against big government has produced hiring freezes throughout the federal government. The greatest need is for individuals with advanced degrees (computer science, biology, health, and agricultural specialties, among others) and in clerical positions. Neither option is suited for those with undergraduate degrees. White-collar entry-level job openings

are limited or nonexistent in most departments (the Department of Defense is a notable exception, but even it is not hiring extensively). Although attitudes and politics may change, the simple fact remains that there is a glut of federal employees. To ease the situation, the jobs of many individuals who leave government service are not being refilled.

But as job opportunities dwindle at the federal level, they are growing at the state and local levels. As Washington, DC, requires these governmental bodies to provide services once handled by federal agencies, administrative and managerial positions are being created.

Geographic Job Index

The Washington, DC, metropolitan area has the highest concentration of federal jobs. Most federal departments and agencies are headquartered either in the city itself or in the Virginia-Maryland suburbs. However, federal offices are spread across the United States. Some offices, such as the Internal Revenue Service and the Federal Bureau of Investigation, are found in every state; others, such as the State Department and the National Archives, have branches in key cities. Military installations often create high numbers of nonmilitary jobs in the areas around them. When applying to the federal government, relocation is an important consideration. Your willingness to move may increase your chances of winning a coveted position.

At the state and local levels, you will find the highest concentrations of jobs in state capitals, county seats, and large cities.

How to Break into the Field

Unlike many other employers, the federal government offers a great deal of aid to job-hunters, but because you are dealing with a bureaucracy, red-tape hassles are unavoidable. Be prepared to be aggressive, assertive, and, above all, patient in your job search.

The place to begin is a Federal Job Information Office (check the Yellow Pages for the nearest location). Here you can learn about the various jobs within the federal government, as well as the current hiring outlook. The information centers have publications called occupational briefs, each of which describes a job in detail. These brochures are also available at libraries, but only at an information center are you sure to get the most recent information.

You should first determine if the position you seek is within the competitive service or the excepted service. Jobs in the competitive service are handled through the federal government's central personnel agency, the Office of Personnel Management. Departments and agencies that hire under the excepted service have their own personnel departments. In either case, you file a basic application called Standard Form 171 and submit an academic transcript. Some departments require additional procedures—written tests, security checks, medical exams, and others. Your qualifications are evaluated, and you are given a numerical rating and placed on a register. When your name appears at the top of the register, your application is submitted to offices that are hiring. If you have not noted any geographic restrictions, you could be considered by any potential federal employer anywhere in the country. You may be interviewed in person or, if the office is distant, over the phone.

An application may be renewed each year by reporting all pertinent work experience. Although work experience can give you an edge over other candidates, a career in government should be started within a few years after graduation. The federal government prefers to promote from within. An outside (or "nonstatus") person will be hired for a management position instead of a government ("status") employee only if the position requires very specific skills.

There are U.S. Government Offices of Personnel Management in Washington, DC, Atlanta, GA, Boston, MA, Chicago, IL, Dallas, TX, Denver, CO, New York, NY, Philadelphia, PA, St. Louis, MO, San Francisco, CA, and Seattle, WA.

State and local governments also have personnel departments. The hiring process may be similar to that of the federal government, but should be less complicated.

Again, the first step is to find out where job information is available and to whom applications must be addressed. Many state and local governments require that their employees reside in the political division, which could be an important consideration in your job search.

International Job Opportunities

In addition to obvious international jobs, such as the foreign service and the Peace Corps, the federal government offers a number of opportunities to work abroad. The Office of Personnel Management and Federal Job Information Centers have information on the types of overseas jobs available and the qualifications. In many instances, competence in a foreign language is preferred or required. (Keep in mind that a large number of these international opportunities are for clerical personnel.)

THE PEACE CORPS

More than 5000 Americans work as Peace Corps volunteers in the developing nations of Africa, Asia, Latin America, and the Pacific. They work on an endless variety of projects—starting a chicken farm, building a road system, working in hospitals or with youth. Americans of any age and background can apply, and many are recent college graduates. All offer their skills as volunteers, making two-year commitments, and serve as guests of the host countries. You may work on projects funded by the United States government, or you may receive funds from other governments or international agencies. You may work with other volunteers—either from the Peace Corps or from other organizations, including non-American ones—or you may be sent on an assignment alone.

Service in the Peace Corps does not mark the beginning of a set career path. Some former volunteers work as administrators with the Peace Corps, but no one serves with this purpose in mind. Instead, individuals apply because of the extraordinary experiences offered. Your courage, endurance, and creativity and your managerial, organizational, and interpersonal skills are tested in situations completely unlike any you have known. You become a friend, teacher, and partner to the people you work with, adapting to their culture and living in the same surroundings. You may find yourself in an isolated mountain village or on a remote South Sea island, surrounded by people who have had limited exposure to Americans. You may have to contend with some resentment to outside intrusion, and you risk your personal safety by living with primitive sanitation and health facilities.

Although the personal rewards should be your primary concern, Peace Corps experience can be a valuable asset if you plan a career in the international sector, whether that career is the foreign service, the United Nations (although opportunities for United States citizens are extremely limited there) or other international organizations, or in international business. It is equally valuable if you plan to teach, do research, or write about global affairs. The experience can also enhance advanced studies in Third World politics, international relations, or global economics.

Applicants are carefully screened by former volunteers. Good intentions are not enough; you should be able to demonstrate some skills in agriculture, construction, nutrition, business, science, or health and community service. Volunteers receive 8 to 12 weeks of training in the United States, which can include a crash course in native language and customs. Usually, volunteers are sent to host countries in groups; however, chances are good that once you arrive you will not be working with other volunteers. You may start a project from scratch, or work in established institutions, such as schools and hospitals.

During your two-year commitment, you receive a modest living allowance, transportation to and from your assignment, and a small compensation (presently $175 per month) that is given you on your return.

For application information, write:

The Peace Corps
806 Connecticut Avenue, N.W.
Washington, DC 20526

INTELLIGENCE SERVICES

The cloak-and-dagger intrigues of spying have given way to satellite photography and reams of computer-generated statistics. The secret agent still serves a purpose, but twentieth-century intelligence gathering has evolved from Mata Hari to modern science. The federal government employs large staffs of skilled people with varied backgrounds, all of whom endeavor to analyze and understand the current world situation.

The two main sources of intelligence gathering for the United States government are the Central Intelligence Agency (CIA) and the less well-known Defense Intelligence Agency (DIA). The CIA reports directly to the president and the National Security Council, providing information on the world situation as it relates to national security. The DIA also investigates international matters, but is responsible for providing information directly to the Department of Defense. Although they serve the military, DIA analysts are nonmilitary personnel. In many respects, both organizations analyze the same data, but the users of this information and their purposes in requesting it are different.

The DIA closely monitors foreign military affairs. The agency assesses the strength and preparedness of foreign armed forces, the types and quantities of their equipment, the movement of these forces, and the new weapons they develop. To complement its understanding of military affairs, the DIA investigates the history,

politics, economics, geography, industrial capability, and resources of a nation. This agency keeps up-to-date information on
foreign military installations, tracks compliance with international
arms agreements, and will, if necessary, investigate the status of
prisoners of war and answer questions about those missing in
action.

The DIA has also become concerned with watching the growth
and activities of international terrorist organizations. The information gathered about these groups is vital to the safety of American
military and foreign service personnel.

The CIA monitors these same areas, but its efforts are not
focused on foreign military affairs. This organization is more
concerned with the political and social situations in other countries. It does not make decisions on how the United States government should react to international events, but provides information
to those officials who do set national policy.

The job of the intelligence analyst in either agency is to gather all
bits of information, which may be fragmentary or secondhand, and
to try to create a coherent image of a nation or a particular
international problem.

The economist's skills are needed to collect and analyze information on a nation's resources, industries, and trade, and its
national and international monetary policies. The soaring debts
and inflation rates of developing nations are producing political
and military repercussions; so the economist is going to play an
increasingly important intelligence role.

In many jobs the ability to speak or read a foreign language is a
valuable asset. For example, the CIA has an entire department
devoted simply to following international news media. Both agencies offer opportunities to work abroad for a part of your career, but
options are available only to experienced personnel.

Both agencies hire outside the Office of Personnel Management. Each subjects applicants to medical exams and stringent
security checks. Many applicants have advanced degrees, but
those with bachelor's degrees are considered. Each agency has an
extensive training program for entry-level personnel.

At the entry level, you are responsible for gathering information from various sources. The more advanced you become, the more you will be involved in analysis. Continuing education is an important part of any intelligence career. Your agency will offer classes that will increase your knowledge and expertise, and you may be required to study at a university or college.

For information on careers in the CIA, write:

Director of Personnel
Central Intelligence Agency
Washington, DC 20505

For information on careers with the DIA, write:

Defense Intelligence Agency
Civilian Personnel Operation Division
Recruitment Office
Washington, DC 20301

FOREIGN SERVICE

The foreign service serves the president and the secretary of state by planning and conducting United States foreign policy. Foreign Service Officers (FSO) work at the State Department in Washington, DC, and in over 230 embassies, missions, and consulates around the world. The foreign service offers an unusually varied career, but the decision to explore this department should not be taken lightly. You will be successful and happy only if you have extraordinary discipline and commitment, and view the benefits as far outweighing the sacrifices.

The foreign service is among the most competitive careers you might explore. Simply getting an offer of a foreign service commission is difficult; throughout a lifetime of service, you can expect to compete against other skilled FSOs for virtually every assignment and promotion.

Obviously, only United States citizens are eligible. You must first sit for the foreign service exam, offered the first Saturday of each December. A broad knowledge of domestic and foreign affairs, with an emphasis on American history, government, and culture, is required. English skills are tested, because an FSO must articulate United States policies. A test of specific skill areas determines the elements of foreign service work best suited to your abilities.

If you pass the test, you are given an all-day oral assessment of your background, temperament, and attitudes. Finally, you must pass a medical exam. With these requirements successfully completed, you are placed on one or more registers, depending on your skills and interests. Each register leads to placement in one of five functional areas: political, economic, administrative, consular, and informational-cultural. The number of openings varies from year to year, but of the approximately 12,000 people who take the test each December, perhaps 300 will eventually be commissioned. The majority of appointees have advanced degrees or work experience or both; their maturity and increased knowledge make the competition even tougher for recent graduates.

If you are accepted into the foreign service, you are given several weeks of orientation at the Foreign Service Institute, followed by up to seven months of training. Fluency in a foreign language is not a requirement for application, but it is an asset. FSOs are instructed in a language, and the length of your training is largely determined by your needs in this area. Your career prospects are enhanced by competence in several languages. The foreign service is particularly interested in applicants who speak Russian, Arabic, Mandarin Chinese, and other languages rarely studied by Americans.

Sixty percent of the average FSO career is spent abroad, and an important prerequisite for application is a willingness to be assigned anywhere. You may be pleased at the thought of working in Hong Kong or Brussels, but how do you feel about Ouagadougou, Port Moresby, and Tegucigalpa? In many parts of the world, respect for diplomatic immunity can no longer be taken for granted, and the threat of international terrorism is forcing embassies to adopt once-unimagined security measures. Personal safety has become an important consideration, especially for officers with families. Regardless of the capacity in which you serve, the most important part of your job is defending and winning support for United States policies, even those contrary to your personal opinions.

There are five principal areas in which you may serve.

Political Affairs: As a political officer, you analyze the political situation in the country to which you are posted, and present United States policies to officials of that nation's government. In Washington, DC, political officers serve in State Department offices that specialize in various regions. They analyze embassy reports, brief government officials, and work with foreign diplomats accredited to Washington.

Economic Affairs: Economic officers stationed abroad interpret United States economic policies while analyzing and reporting on foreign economies. To understand a nation's economy, the officer studies local finances, trade, resources, and industries. In Washington, DC, economic officers contribute to the formulation of national and international economic policies.

If you do well in the economic portion of the foreign service exam, you may also be considered for appointment to the Foreign Commercial Service. Here you work under the direction of the Department of Commerce rather than the Department of State. The Foreign Commercial Service Officer is stationed abroad and seeks to promote trade between the United States and a foreign nation. The job involves a great deal of work with local business and government officials, so language skills are extremely important.

Administrative Affairs: Overseas, administrative officers are concerned with daily operations of embassies and consulates, such as personnel, budgeting, security, and communications. In Washington, DC, they provide support for those stationed abroad.

Consular Services: Here you work closely with the public, both American citizens and foreign nationals, by dealing with passport, visa, and immigration concerns. Foreign language skills are extremely important. Consular officers are stationed in embassies and consulates, which are located in key foreign cities. In Washington, DC, the Bureau of Consular Affairs provides support for consular officers abroad with guidance and aid in problem situations.

United States International Communication Agency: This agency strives to give foreign people an understanding of American culture, attitudes, institutions, and values. Service as a foreign service information officer means getting to know a foreign society while explaining our own by importing and disseminating American art, films, and journalism. You might also be involved in organizing educational and cultural exchange programs. An important part of your job will be to invite American lecturers, performers, and athletes to visit the country in which you are stationed. Information officers in Washington, DC, help to coordinate these visits.

Career Paths

Your career path will vary with the changing policies and needs of the State Department. You are reassigned at intervals of two to four years, often alternating an overseas posting with a stay in Washington, DC. However, assignments are entirely dependent on your skills and where they can best be used at any given time. Experienced FSOs are expected to specialize in a function, such as political affairs or consular services. However, in practice, most FSOs perform a variety of jobs. Officers are ranked, and promotions depend on annual ratings.

An ambassadorship is publicly perceived as the highest foreign service post. However, in reality, most United States ambassadors are political appointees who have little or no foreign service experience. Some skilled FSOs reach the level of senior foreign service officers. These may be appointed as ambassadors, but most senior officers remain in the United States, guiding State Department policies and programs.

For information on foreign service careers, write:

Foreign Service Management
Officer Recruitment Branch
P.O. Box 9317
Rosslyn Station
Arlington, VA 22209

ADDITIONAL INFORMATION

Salaries

Although governmental bodies often pay their employees less than private industries, they offer attractive perks. Government employees receive generous vacation and sick leave, exceptional benefits, and pension and early retirement plans.

Most federal employees, including those of the CIA and the DIA, are paid according to a standard pay schedule. Each promotion is accompanied by a change of GS rating. The typical graduate is hired as a GS-5 or GS-7, depending on academic record and work experience. A graduate degree holder is hired at GS-9. In the foreign service, the pay schedule is comparable to that in other government jobs, but varies according to the nation in which you are stationed. Foreign Service Officers in many countries receive hardship pay and/or living allowances.

The following chart gives the federal white-collar annual pay schedule as of January 1, 1984 (figures are the lowest wages for each GS rating).

GS1	$ 8,980	GS10	$23,088
GS2	$10,097	GS11	$25,366
GS3	$11,017	GS12	$30,402
GS4	$12,367	GS13	$36,152
GS5	$13,837	GS14	$42,722
GS6	$15,423	GS15	$50,252
GS7	$17,138	GS16	$58,938
GS8	$18,981	GS17	$69,042
GS9	$20,965	GS18	$80,920

Extracurricular Activities/Work Experience

Model United Nations
Student Government
Participation in a language house or organizations that
investigate other cultures
Writing for campus publications, particularly those that
deal with national and international affairs

Internships

The federal government sponsors an excellent program of cooperative education for undergraduates. However, for you to be eligible, your college must participate in the program.

Students from a wide variety of majors are recruited to work full-time or part-time at a government agency. Most positions are for those with a specific academic concentration, such as accounting and computer science. Students with other backgrounds can find openings, but opportunities are more limited. For information, consult your school's internship or placement office.

The Department of State offers plenty of options for students interested in a foreign service career. You may be a summer intern, which is a paying position, or you may intern during a fall or spring semester, which is not compensated. Applications for a summer position must be submitted by the preceding November 1; applications for a fall or spring internship must be received at least six months in advance. Students must be juniors or seniors, have studied some pertinent coursework, and be willing to permit a background investigation before they are accepted.

For information, write:

Intern Coordinator
Department of State
P.O. Box 9317
Rosslyn Station
Arlington, VA 22209-0317

Recommended Reading

BOOKS

American Foreign Policy by Henry Kissinger, W.W. Norton: 1977

Caveat: Realism, Reagan and Foreign Policy by Alexander Haig, Macmillan Publishing Company: 1984

Dictatorships and Double Standards: Rationalism and Realism in Politics by Jeanne Kirkpatrick, Simon and Schuster: 1982

Hard Choices: Four Critical Years in Managing America's Foreign Policy by Cyrus Vance, Simon and Schuster: 1983

World Almanac Book of Facts, World Almanac: 1984

PERIODICALS

Department of State Bulletin (monthly), United States Department of State, Washington, DC 20520

Development Digest (quarterly), United States Department of State, Agency for International Development, United States Government Printing Office, Superintendent of Documents, Washington, DC 20402

Foreign Affairs (bimonthly), 58 East 68th Street, New York, NY 10021

Foreign Service Journal (weekly), Foreign Service Association, 2101 E Street, N.W., Washington, DC 20037

Government Employee Relations Report (weekly), The Bureau of National Affairs, 1231 25th Street, Washington, DC 20037

State (monthly), United States Department of State, United States Government Printing Office, Superintendent of Documents, Washington, DC 20402

Professional Associations

American Council of Voluntary Agencies for Foreign
    Service
200 Park Avenue South
New York, NY 10003

American Foreign Policy Institute
1101 17th Street, N.W.
Suite 1000
Washington, DC 20036

National Committee on American Foreign Policy
200 Park Avenue
Suite 4416
New York, NY 10017

INTERVIEWS

Edwin Jorge
Recruiter and Former Volunteer
Peace Corps, New York, NY

Before I joined the Peace Corps, I had worked my way up to vice president of a nonprofit organization that dealt with economic development for minorities. I had been aware of the Peace Corps since its inception, and in 1979 I decided that I was financially secure enough to leave my job and become a volunteer.

Because I was born in the Caribbean, I wanted to be posted to that part of the world. I was sent to Jamaica as a community development specialist. I went with the intention of doing something to help the children of Jamaica. I started off with $2000 in seed money from the Canadian government and with it I started programs to get delinquent boys off the streets. We taught them math and English and eventually started a vocational program in auto mechanics. The Street Corner Boys' Program, as it was called, grew to include a medical and dental program and, finally, a hot lunch program. In addition to the Canadian donation, I received funds from the Dutch government and some Norwegian expatriates, and the assistance of Mitzi Seaga, the wife of the prime minister. By the time I left Kingston, that initial $2000 had grown to a total operating budget of over $150,000, including gifts-in-kind. I enjoyed my work and was satisfied that I had accomplished a lot of what I had set out to do. As far as I know, these programs are still operating.

When I finished my two years, I knew I wanted to stay with the Peace Corps and that I wanted to recruit. I felt I had a good idea of what makes a good volunteer, and I wanted to contribute to the Corps by ensuring that only the best people are sent abroad. Because of what I had accomplished in Kingston, I was given an excellent recommendation and moved directly into recruiting.

I interview candidates and decide if they have what it takes to be volunteers. A recruiter has to be an excellent judge of character, because there is no lack of applicants. Each candidate is assigned to a recruiter. If I get someone who is well qualified, it is my responsibility to get that person to make a commitment and volunteer.

We are especially interested in finding people who have been involved in the community. We also like to see some demonstrated interest in the Third World, but that is not an absolute requirement. The key to being accepted is proving that you want to work with people and that you will be able to live in another culture.

To be quite honest, the Peace Corps is the best job I've ever had. I love it. When I made the decision to become a recruiter, I took a cut in salary that left me with half of what I was making when I went into the Corps as a volunteer. I wouldn't change that decision for anything.

Stephanie Smith Kinney, Age 40
Foreign Service Officer; Uruguay/Paraguay Desk, Bureau
of Inter-American Affairs
Department of State, Washington, DC

My interest in the foreign service goes back a long way. I first investigated it in high school and my research had discouraging results. At that time, I discovered, a foreign service career was difficult for women. Female officers did not go beyond mid-level positions, married women weren't accepted, and if a female officer married, an unwritten rule compelled her to resign.

But I kept my long-standing interest in the rest of the world. At Vassar, I majored in Spanish literature and Latin American affairs. I spent my junior year at the University of Madrid. I was interested in teaching, so I went on for a master's in education at Harvard.

The foreign service reentered my life when my husband became a foreign service officer about a year after we were married. His first assignment was Mexico City, which he accepted at my instigation. I wanted to be in a Spanish-speaking country because I thought I could use my background. I experienced the difficulty of being a foreign service spouse when I found that restrictions prevented me from working. I fought the regulations and became the first United States foreign service spouse officially permitted to work in Mexico City.

When we returned to Washington in 1974 we were faced with a choice: sacrifice my desire for a career, my husband's career, or our marriage. I decided the easiest option was to try to change the system in which my husband worked. I became part of a group that was working to get the State Department to be more concerned with the problems of foreign service spouses and families.

I finally decided that the best way to fight the foreign service was to join it (married women were no longer excluded), and I passed the exam and the orals and was accepted as an officer in 1976. One of my first assignments was as a management analyst charged with looking into family issues and "solving the growing spouse problems." I was a key force in creating the Family Liaison Office, the headquarters of which was inaugurated in the State Department in March 1977. Today, it has 92 branches overseas which help family members deal with the myriad problems posed by their highly mobile, international life-style.

From that start I've done a variety of things. I'm in the administrative function or "cone," but I've never had a truly administrative job. Now I'm on a political desk, Uruguay and Paraguay. Before that, I was with the United States Information Agency in New York. I served as assistant science attaché and also did consular and press work in Rome, and I worked in cultural affairs for West Africa in the Department.

The best and the most successful people rarely conform to structure—if you're creative, you cut your own path. My own career has been a combination of coincidence and necessity. My husband and I try to coordinate our assignments, but we must always apply individually. If a couple is not given assignments at the same post, they may take separate assignments or one spouse may take leave without pay.

If you are considering a career in the foreign service, you must be a generalist: have a background in American culture and history, economics, public administration, and political analysis. You should be confident that you can learn a foreign language. Some experience abroad is an asset—if only because it proves you can work in another culture. You must have a sense of conviction about the United States—a sense of what we are and what we should be—and a willingness to serve it. On the personal side, you must have social graces (or a willingness to learn them), a high tolerance for frustration, a sense of adventure, optimism, and a sense of humor. Although you play a defined role in a tradition-bound profession, what enables you to perform is your own sense of purpose.

It is important that you think through your priorities and your needs as a person. What do you want in a career? Do you want marriage? Children? It is difficult enough to combine a family and a career when you stay in one place—it's that much more difficult in a highly mobile career. People often see only the glamour and excitement of foreign service life—to the exclusion of the drudgery, danger, and sacrifice it can also require. It's not just a job, it's a total commitment—so it's better not to approach it with any illusions.

HOTEL
MANAGEMENT

BEHIND the scenes of bustling hotel lobbies, elegant resorts, and well-appointed conference centers are large staffs with a wide and varied range of skills. Salespeople, managers, dietitians, tour packagers, housekeepers—there is a place for these and numerous others in this colorful and challenging industry.

The hotel industry is growing and changing. Cities and regions are promoting tourism as a source of revenue. More foreigners are traveling in the United States. Hotel chains have expanded in the past ten years, both in the United States and abroad. These developments have increased the competition for travelers' dollars and have created countless new jobs. New challenges have been added to many career positions. Hotels can no longer depend on their size and location for custom; they must actively promote and sell their services. Thus, sales, marketing, advertising, and public relations have become as vital as traditional hotel services.

If you're a take-charge person who enjoys planning and supervising, and can juggle the potentially conflicting demands of gracious service and efficient operations, the industry will welcome you. The chance to live and work in different locales appeals to many candidates. Liberal arts and business graduates will find that they can apply their education and personal qualities in:

- **Front House Operations**
- **Food and Beverage Services**
- **Sales and Marketing**

Few people have trouble finding entry-level jobs, and most of these positions lead quickly to better ones if you show initiative and take extra training. Newcomers, however, must be prepared to put in long hours and learn many facets of the trade. On the plus side, there's plenty of opportunity to take on added responsibility and move up the ladder in a variety of ways. Many hotel chains, independent hotels, and resort facilities offer on-the-job training programs that provide the opportunity for liberal arts and business majors to advance and compete with graduates with degrees in hotel and restaurant management.

Like most service-oriented industries, hotels and resorts are dynamic businesses. New technology has aready meant that room reservations and financial operations are computerized. Teleconferencing is changing the nature of the convention and conferences areas of the industry, although its impact is not yet clear. This new means of communication is expected to be a strong factor in attracting business clients. Hotels that specialize in conventions may lose room sales because of teleconferencing; on the other hand, both large and smaller hotels that host teleconferences may well develop additional business.

Job Outlook

Jobs Openings Will Grow: Faster than average

Competition for Jobs: Minimal

New Job Opportunities: The concierge, a standby of European service, is beginning to appear in America's better urban hotels.

There are few positions now, but the opportunities are expected to grow. The concierge knows a city inside out, has contacts everywhere, and provides special assistance to guests. A concierge might obtain tickets to a sold-out show, recommend a nearby optician, or locate a boutique with bilingual personnel. This job requires ingenuity and confidence. No training is available, but if the idea appeals to you, you might be able to create such a position for yourself, once you have worked at the front desk and become familiar with the problems and requests that arise. You'd do well to consult a concierge at a major hotel, who may be able to offer some tips on persuading management to let you try your hand.

Geographic Job Index

Hotels of course, are found everywhere. The largest, and some of the most prestigious, are located in and around major convention and tourist centers, such as San Francisco, CA, Miami, FL, Atlanta, GA, Chicago, IL, New York, NY, and Washington, DC. Other important hotels are in resort areas. If you are interested in moving regularly, big domestic and international chains offer the best opportunities for relocation.

Who the Employers Are

HOTEL CHAINS are national and international corporations that operate a number of establishments. They offer many customer services and have a multi-tiered management structure. Chains provide good opportunities for advancement, transfer, and travel. Because employees are transferred frequently, you have a better chance of being promoted quickly than you would in an independent hotel. Corporate headquarters jobs, in, for example, marketing, usually go to employees with experience or advanced degrees or both.

MOTELS are smaller establishments than hotels. They normally provide fewer services, and as a result do not offer as many job opportunities. However, motels located within major cities often do provide services approaching those of hotels, and large motel chains employ marketing and sales personnel at their corporate headquarters.

Major Employers

HOTEL CHAINS

Americana Hotels Corporation, Chicago, IL
Dunfey Hotels, Hampton, NH
Fairmount Hotel Company, San Francisco, CA
Four Seasons Hotels Ltd., Toronto, ON
Helmsley Hotels, New York, NY
Hilton Hotels Corporation, Beverly Hills, CA
Hyatt Corporation, Rosemont, IL
Meridien Hotels, New York, NY
The Sheraton Corporation, Boston, MA
Westin Hotel Company, Seattle, WA

MOTEL CHAINS

Best Western International, Phoenix, AZ
Holiday Inns, Inc., Memphis, TN
Howard Johnson Company, Boston, MA
Marriott Corporation, Bethesda, MD
Ramada Inns, Inc., Phoenix, AZ

How to Break into the Field

Finding an entry-level job is not too difficult, especially in the service-oriented departments (food service and house management). A résumé and cover letter to the manager of the department that interests you, the same information to the personnel department, and a follow-up call is the way to start. You will be competing with graduates of hotel/restaurant management training programs. The more challenging entry-level positions often go to people with this targeted education. You must demonstrate your willingness to learn the hotel business from the bottom up.

To become familiar with hotel work and to make contacts, find out from the local convention bureau when large conventions are coming to town and where they will be headquartered. Then contact the hotel and offer to work part-time on the front desk during the convention. You might also make advance contact with convening associations and offer to help in the hospitality booth or in the press room. In addition, a hotel may also need extra help during peak seasons.

International Job Opportunities

Possibilities for overseas work exist in the international hotel chains, but you need to prove your competence in the United States first. If you are fluent in a foreign language and have several years of front desk experience, you have a good chance of being transferred abroad.

FRONT DESK OPERATIONS

The hotel personnel with whom guests come into personal contact comprise the so-called front of the house. They include the door attendant, the bellhop, and the front desk clerk, as well as the individuals who supervise their activities. They play a key role in the hotel's image, and because repeat business is vital to the industry, they must provide consistently excellent service.

Often called the nerve center, the front desk handles the needs of the guests from arrival to check-out. This experience gives the desk clerk a good understanding of the hotel's customers and what they expect in the way of service. Also, the desk clerk learns to cooperate with other employees in the common purpose of efficiently and readily meeting the guests' needs.

Traditionally, the front house has been the starting place for employees whose sights are set on becoming general manager—the executive responsible for all the activities of the hotel. With desk experience behind you, you are able to direct a variety of large staffs and set policies concerning the inner workings of the hotel.

The general manager was once concerned primarily with the needs of the average guest. This concern is still important, but the general manager's responsibilities have now become so broad that supervisors from the sales or the beverage and food divisions can move into this top position. The ideal general manager is one who has had supervisory experience in all areas of the hotel business.

The front desk is still the best place to start if you plan to move into top management, but you must be prepared to seize every opportunity to expand the depth and breadth of your experience within the entire industry.

There is no set career path from the entry-level position to the top because each hotel or chain has its own departmental divisions and personnel structures. Before moving into a mid-management position, almost any candidate would go through a six-month to one-year training program. After that, hotel employees might spend up to six years in various supervisory assistantships before earning a more elevated title. The length of time in each position varies according to the size and structure of the hotel or chain, and your willingness and ability to move into new areas.

Qualifications

Personal: Energetic. A friendly disposition. A sense of diplomacy. Self-assurance. Common sense. The ability to make quick decisions and to work independently.

Professional: Clerical skills. Bookkeeping may be helpful.

Career Paths

LEVEL	JOB TITLE	EXPERIENCE NEEDED
Entry	Front desk clerk or room clerk	College degree
2	Assistant manager, front office	2-4 years
3	Senior manager, front office	4-6 years
4	Rooms division supervisor	7-10 years

| 5 | Assistant hotel manager | 15 + years |
| 6 | General manager | 20 + years |

Job Responsibilities

Entry Level

THE BASICS: Take reservations. Assign rooms. Register guests. Handle room keys. Answer questions. Relay messages.

MORE CHALLENGING DUTIES: Supervising clerks, cashiers, and night auditors. Training personnel.

Moving Up

After you have proven your commitment, learned basic hotel operations, and gained an understanding of the guests' needs, you will be an ideal candidate for assistant manager in the front office. Your promotion will come more quickly if you have from time to time taken the initiative to gain extra responsibility and experience. The assistant acts as a liaison between the desk clerks and the front office manager. As front office manager, you spend most of your time directing your personnel, but handling major complaints from customers remains an inescapable part of the job. Depending on the size and structure of the hotel, you might move into other supervisory positions, such as rooms division supervisor, in charge of reservations and housekeeping. As you become qualified for higher level management jobs, you may well find that your chances of reaching that level are improved if you change employers.

FOOD AND BEVERAGE SERVICES

Conventions, banquets, conferences, and other group affairs are important sources of a hotel's income. This department arranges everything from wedding receptions and high school proms to major business, political, or social gatherings involving hundreds or even thousands of guests. The responsibilities include scheduling the events, assigning physical facilities, planning and arranging meals and such special services as additional security, extra staff, and press accommodations. The convention and banquet services department stage manages these events, cooperating closely with the customer's representatives—a job that might be purely simple and routine or a herculean task.

The department is also in charge of the hotel's dining rooms, bars, and coffeeshops, which are open to the public and operated as any independent restaurant or cocktail lounge. Managing these facilities requires close and constant supervision of a large and active staff of waiters, chefs, and others.

Duties are extremely varied in this department. Working here gives you an excellent grounding in business management, supervision of extensive staff, and dealing with emergencies smoothly and with dispatch. You must be very well organized, almost unflappable, and able to keep several balls in the air at once.

If you do not have a hotel/restaurant management degree and you aspire to a mid-managerial position in a large hotel, you would have to enter a training program to learn the responsibilities of the kitchen steward, the chef, and the purchasing manager, and their staffs. Career paths vary greatly. They depend on the size and number of the hotel's facilities, and on your own talents and plans.

Qualifications

Personal: Outgoing, energetic personality. Creativity. Appreciation of customer's tastes. Organizational ability. Ability to think on your feet.

Professional: Business knowledge. Familiarity with kitchen and dining room procedures. Ability to uphold standards of quality on a daily basis.

Career Paths

LEVEL	JOB TITLE	EXPERIENCE NEEDED
Entry	Trainee	College degree
2	Assistant supervisor of food, beverage, or banquet division	6 months-1 year
3	Supervisor	3-5 years
4	Assistant to food and beverage director	6-8 years
5	Food and beverage director	10-15+ years

Job Responsibilities

Entry Level

THE BASICS: Assigning table-seating arrangements. Learning the menu. Handling last-minute problems.

MORE CHALLENGING DUTIES: Booking groups. Suggesting menus for group functions. Planning logistics. Developing budgets and marketing and advertising strategies.

Moving Up

After you understand the operations of a particular area (banquet services, for example) you move up to assistant supervisor and begin to train for a management position. Your basic function will be assisting your supervisor, but you will be using salesmanship as well to help promote the restaurant or the banquet and convention facilities with special deals and advertising. An ability to deal effectively and quickly with the needs and grievances of guests and clients is paramount.

After two or three years you would advance to supervisor, managing personnel and coordinating your division. In most major hotels, food services, beverage services, and banquet services are separate, although interrelated functions.

If you have food service experience and have proven your managerial skills, you might choose to work in catering services. The catering manager works closely with groups and associations, serving their special needs. You may provide something as simple as a small wine and cheese reception or as elaborate as a five-course banquet.

With a solid background of experience, you are eligible for advancement to assistant director and director of food and beverage services, supervising this entire division of the hotel. These jobs involve the overseeing of personnel, purchasing and inventory control, monitoring cleanliness and quality, and some advertising and promotion.

Moving up requires a demonstration of initiative—visiting competitors, for example, seeing their methods, and getting ideas to improve your own operations. Because food and beverage services, like front house operations, is a service-oriented function, the customers are everything. Talk with them, discover their needs, listen to their complaints and compliments, and apply what you learn.

MARKETING/SALES

An increased emphasis on this function goes hand-in-hand with the growing competition among hotel chains. The marketing and sales department is responsible for many of the special offers and promotions that attract guests. For example, many hotels have devised schemes to draw business travelers—everything from discounts to free breakfasts and complimentary copies of *The Wall Street Journal*. It is especially important that hotels attract large travel groups and conventions because these are important sources of income. Salespeople are responsible for presenting an appealing package to these potential clients. Often just selling the hotel is not enough—you must also sell its location and special features. Although the hotel may have exceptional facilities, it is competing with many others of comparable quality. Local amenities, atmosphere, and convenience to transportation are discussed along with cost and the client's individual needs. Using these starting points, you must hit on a way to present your hotel and your city persuasively. Creativity, flexibility, and the power to persuade are the keys to success.

Recent graduates enter this department as sales trainees. Once you have an overview of the hotel and convention industries (which might take several months), you become an account executive and start working with clients.

Qualifications

Personal: Energetic, sociable personality. Ability to persuade others. Analytic skills. Insight into human nature. Persistence.

Professional: Business sense. Aptitude for numbers. Knowledge of computers and teleconferencing helpful but not essential. Sales or public relations experience often preferred.

Career Paths

LEVEL	JOB TITLE	EXPERIENCE NEEDED
Entry	Sales trainee	College degree
2	Account executive	6 months-1 year
3	Group sales manager	3-7 years
4	Area sales manager	10+ years
5	Marketing and sales manager	15+ years

Job Reponsibilities

Entry Level

THE BASICS: Calling on associations, large groups, and travel agencies to interest them in the facility you represent. Maintaining accounts. Representing your hotel/resort and city at trade shows. Analyzing your facility and the competition. Giving tours of your hotel.

MORE CHALLENGING DUTIES: Handling group sales. Creating and presenting bids. Overseeing marketing plans and advertising. Writing promotional literature.

Moving Up

As an account executive, you'll start with local groups and work up to handling national organizations, whose needs are more complex. The group sales manager supervises the account executives and is in charge of dealing with more prestigious associations and groups.

The area sales manager handles a particular territory, which in sales language is a specific type of organization—sports, youth, trade associations.

The marketing/sales manager is in charge of the entire department and approves the bids created by the account executives. It takes experience and some daring to set a price that is high enough to be profitable yet lower than the competition's. You must be sure, as well, that the hotel can deliver all the promised services. Hotel marketing and sales managers often work with tourist bureaus and local government officials to promote their city or region.

To move up, you must cope with different personalities and deal with office and city politics. You also need confidence, a fresh outlook, and the knowledge of costs and contingencies that equips you to create competitive bids. In this department, the most successful professionals are those with the personality and persistence to sell the hotel, the city, and, above all, themselves.

ADDITIONAL INFORMATION

Salaries

It is difficult to characterize salaries in the hotel industry because pay is determined by the size, prestige, and location of the hotel. Perks, such as discounts on meals, discounts at chain-affiliated hotels (if you work in the chain), bonuses, and profit-sharing plans, add to your base pay. General managers and, less often, other top managers may receive housing.

Entry-level salaries vary widely—from $10,000 to $20,000 a year. The highest salaries usually go to graduates of hotel/restaurant management programs. Front house personnel also tend to be better paid than those in other departments.

An assistant departmental manager may earn between $20,000 and $35,000 a year; a departmental manager may earn between $30,000 and $60,000 a year. The general managers of the most prestigious urban hotels may receive compensations exceeding $70,000.

Working Conditions

Hours: In front house operations and food and beverage services, expect changing shifts that include night hours and weekend work. The hours in these sections of the industry are never routine because the hotel and its banquet facilities are open beyond normal business hours. Management personnel in both areas are used to overtime; they may work a 70-hour week during a major convention. The marketing and sales department tends to keep regular hours, although overtime is common as you adapt your working hours to your clients' needs.

Environment: The desk clerk is in public view most of the time, stationed at the reception desk. Front house managers have offices, but the nature of your work will keep you moving throughout the hotel a great deal of the time. In banquet services, the restaurant becomes a second home. Food services personnel have offices, but these are often small and not far from the noise of the kitchen and the restaurant. In sales and marketing, entry-level personnel often share work space, but since it is removed from the public areas of the hotel the work environment is quieter and less hectic that in front house or food and beverage services.

Workstyle: Your job as a desk clerk means that you are in extensive and continual contact with guests, both over the phone and face-to-face. At peak times, such as morning check-out, the pace can be hectic. Evening hours tend to be calmer. In banquet services, you will be consistently on the move: supervising staff, meeting customers, making arrangements, and showing the hotel's facilities. Sales and marketing are desk jobs. In sales, expect a great deal of phone work and many meetings.

Travel: In national chains, opportunities exist for management personnel in all areas to visit member hotels to exchange ideas and experiences. Sales and marketing personnel could travel nationally (and even internationally) in their quest to attract convention, tour groups, and other new business, but not usually at entry level. Management personnel, particularly in sales, can be temporarily moved to newly opened hotels to help their staffs begin functioning.

Hotel chains often try to foster an international image, so temporary assignments overseas are not uncommon for desk clerks who speak a foreign language. Such experience can speed your progress in hotels with large foreign clienteles.

Extracurricular Activities/Work Experience

Work at a campus pub, student center or cafeteria

Part-time work in a hotel, restaurant or catering business

Planning social functions for dorms, fraternities,
sororities, and clubs

For sales and marketing: Selling ads for school
   publications

Part time sales work

Internships

Most formal internship programs offered by hotels are geared
primarily toward students majoring in hotel management. Therefore, you must investigate internship possibilities on your own and
must convince prospective sponsors that you are sincerely interested in a hotel career and can be useful to their operation. Your
chances of being accepted as an intern in front desk operations or
banquet facilities are improved if you have hotel or restaurant
experience. Even a stint as a part-time waiter is valuable if it gives
you a chance to observe the operation of a quality restaurant. If you
are interested in an internship in sales and marketing, be sure to
play up sales experience you have had in any area.

Recommended Reading

BOOKS

The American Hotel and Motel Red Book, The American
Hotel and Motel Association. This annual directory lists all
American hotels and motels by city and state.

Directory of Hotel Systems, The American Hotel and Motel
Association. This annual directory lists hotel chains and their
properties.

PERIODICALS

Lodging and Food-Service News (monthly), 131 Clarendon
Street, Boston, MA 02116

Lodging Hospitality (monthly), 111 Chester Avenue, Cleveland, OH 44114

Professional Associations

American Hotel and Motel Association
888 Seventh Avenue
New York, NY 10019

Council on Hotel, Restaurant, and Institutional Education
Human Development Building
Room 118
University Park, PA 16802

Educational Institute of the American Hotel and Motel
    Association
1407 South Harrison Road
Suite 310
EastLansing, MI 32084

National Institute for the Food Service Industry
20 North Wacker Drive
Suite 2620
Chicago, IL 60606

INTERVIEWS

Susan Donahue, Age 28
Director of Sales and Marketing
Meridien Hotels, Boston, MA

I majored in marketing at the University of New Hampshire
because I wanted to go into sales. After graduation I was hired by
the Dunfey Corporation and went through its year-long training
program. I was assigned to sales, the department that interested
me, and began as an entry-level account executive. After I was
rotated through various departments to acquire a general knowledge of the hotel, I began going out on calls with an experienced
salesperson. Once I had the right style and approach, I went out on
my own.

My first job was at the Berkshire Place, a Dunfey hotel in New York City. I advanced to a group sales manager and then became tour and travel sales manager. I then moved to Boston, and became a sales manager with Meridien Hotels, and have since been promoted to my present position.

What makes hotel sales different from many other types of sales is that the product you are selling is intangible—it's your company's services and its name. Now, as the director of sales and marketing, I do some market research. I look into who our clientele has been and what type of customers our competitors are going after. Before opening a hotel in a new city, we have to find out such things as what kind of customers we can attract and where the best location is for our hotel. Once we determine that, we try to contact potential clients so that they're aware of our new facility.

To get into the marketing and sales department of a hotel, you must have good organizational skills, an eye for detail, and strong interpersonal skills. That doesn't necessarily mean you have to have a hotel background. The kind of degree you have is less important than the skills you bring to the job.

Despite the image, I wouldn't say that hotel sales is glamorous work, but it is never dull. Everyone in sales has to put in a lot of work—we work weekends and travel often. Sometimes we are dealing with a lot of money, so there's a high excitement level. I especially like the travel that my own work requires and the frequent interaction with people.

On a typical day I devote much of my time to handling our hotel's largest accounts. I keep in touch with them and make phone calls to potential customers. This kind of work demands an aptitude for numbers as well as an understanding of the customer's needs and of how our hotel meets these needs. During the day I do most of my work over the phone and at business luncheons (I often attend as many as four luncheons a week). I usually prepare sales presentations and reports after hours.

As in any profession, you have to deal with a certain amount of politics to get ahead, but in the long run it is your commitment to the job and your selling ability that pays off.

Karen Dobell, Age 31
Assistant Front Office Manager
The Drake Hotel, Chicago, IL

When I graduated from the University of New Brunswick with a degree in French literature in 1973, I had no idea of what I wanted to do. When I finally started job hunting, I applied to jobs in radio, film, airlines and hotels. I fell into hotels by accident, because the industry tends to make hiring decisions very quickly. Sometimes you hear on the same day you interview. Nevertheless, a hotel job appealed to me. I wanted a job that was different from the usual nine-to-five routine and one in which I could work with people.

I started at the Queen Elizabeth Hotel in Montreal, which is part of Hilton International, in April 1974. I didn't have a formal training period. I started out by working three days a week as an interviewer in the personnel department and two days as a hostess in the coffeeshop. They were using me to fill holes wherever someone was needed. After a summer in these jobs, I spent a month in catering, a month in public relations, and several months in food and beverage. These were all clerical jobs, but I learned a lot. In April 1975 I became a room clerk, and I stayed at the front desk about a year.

In June 1975 I changed employers. A new Four Seasons hotel was opening in Montreal. A friend who had gone to work there lured me over. Three weeks after that hotel opened, the executive housekeeper left and I was given the job. With no experience in housekeeping, I found myself in charge of keeping the hotel clean—which meant directing the staff, hiring new people, seeing the salespeople who promoted cleaning products, testing these products, and so on.

In August 1977 I went to the Queen Elizabeth Hotel because I missed working for Hilton. I went into the sales department as a meetings coordinator, handling smaller conferences held at the hotel. I then moved up to convention coordinator, handling conventions of 800 rooms with as many as 2000 people.

I was transferred to the Harbour Castle Hilton Hotel in Toronto, staying in convention services at first and then becoming sales manager. I was working with the Canadian market only, which is relatively small. We kept files on all associations in the country, and I solicited their business.

In the summer of 1981 I was transferred to Chicago as sales manager of the Drake Hotel. However, I found the American market to be more competitive, especially at that time, when the recession was hurting the convention business. And my personality is such that I wasn't comfortable going to cocktail parties—which is where a lot of sales take place—trying to sell the hotel's services and being aggressive. I fondly remembered my days in the front office: the action, the endless variety, the cohesiveness among the staff. It's the center of things. So I requested a change and became assistant front office manager, a job I still hold.

I think the front desk is really the best place to start in this business. Rooms are what hotels are all about and are what makes this business different from any other. Also, rooms are usually the greatest revenue-producing center for a hotel, so it's important to have a good understanding of how the front desk works.

In the past ten years, I've seen a greater emphasis put on hotel degrees, but anyone can enter this business; it may just take longer if you don't have a specialized degree. The people who do best in this business are the ones who like people, are easy-going, and don't get ruffled easily.

INSURANCE

E VER since James Bolter, a resident of Hartford, Connecticut, paid a two-cent premium for a $1000 policy to the Travelers Insurance Company in 1864, protecting him against physical mishaps on his daily walk to the post office a few blocks away, Americans have been insuring themselves and their possessions. In fact, about 90 percent of Americans today have some form of insurance—health, life, home, or auto.

The scope and direction of American insurance companies have changed considerably since Mr. Bolter paid his two pennies. Today the industry, usually divided into two sectors—health and life, and property and casualty—is concerned not only with individuals but with large and small groups of people as well. It offers protection for almost any condition that might arise, including industrial pollution, nuclear accidents, malpractice, kidnapping, crop failures, and libel.

Despite trying economic conditions during the early 1980s, the need for insurance coverage continued to grow. In the property and casualty sector, approximately $104 billion was spent for premiums, and this figure is expected to reach more than $300 billion by the year 2000.

At present, Americans own more than $3 trillion worth of life insurance. They and their employers pay more than $111 billion per year for health care coverage. What this all adds up to is a very healthy people-oriented industry with many career opportunities for talented, enterprising, and industrious individuals.

Even during the recessionary period of the early 1980s, employment in the industry increased approximately 4 percent, without taking into account an estimated 270,000 people in 1982 who worked as independent agents or were staff employees of such agencies. Looking at casualty/property and health/life separately, the employee growth rate was 20 percent and 8 percent respectively for the period between 1981 and 1982.

Although technology as well as the faltering economy has been responsible for a "compression" in number of clerical and secretarial jobs, the need remains strong in the following areas:

- **Sales**
- **Actuarial**
- **Underwriting**

This is partly because Americans tend not to cut back on insurance coverage even during recessionary periods, and because there will be more Americans between the ages of 25 and 55 who will need coverage.

There is encouraging news for women seeking careers in the insurance industry, too. Data from the Equal Opportunity Commission show that 42 percent of all professional positions in the insurance industry in 1981 were held by women. In 1970, it was 16.9 percent. A total of 26 percent of employees classified as managers or company officials in 1981 were women; only 11 percent of those positions were filled by women in 1970.

Job Outlook

Job Openings Will Grow: As fast as average

Competition for Jobs: Average

Because insurance is not a glamour industry, there is not usually an overabundance of applicants. Many major insurance companies are eager to train ambitious liberal arts or business administration majors at company expense.

New Job Opportunities: Because government deregulation has allowed many insurance companies to offer financial services as well as insurance, individuals with a background in financial planning will be needed to advise and counsel clients. Also, as insurance becomes perhaps the most important of all fringe benefits employees receive, more companies will use the services of insurance consultants and financial planners to select insurance, annuities, and pension plans.

Geographic Job Index

Although insurance agencies are found in almost all communities, large or small, major insurance companies are primarily located in the eastern corridor—Boston, MA, New York, NY, Philadelphia, PA, and Washington, DC. Other U.S. cities with a large concentration of insurance companies are Milwaukee, WI, Chicago, IL, Indianapolis, IN, Dallas, TX, and San Francisco, CA.

Who the Employers Are

The best chances for entry-level positions are often at the home offices of large firms where extensive training programs are available for newcomers. Many of these firms actively recruit on college campuses and advertise in the annual *Insurance Careers,* a magazine supplied to college placement offices.

Major Employers

Aetna Life and Casualty Company, Hartford, CT
Allstate Insurance Company, Northbrook, IL
Equitable Life Assurance Society, New York, NY
Group Health Association of America, Inc., Washington, DC

Hartford Insurance Group, Hartford, CT
Insurance Company of North America, Philadelphia, PA
Liberty Mutual, Boston, MA
Massachusetts Mutual Life Insurance Company, New
York, NY
Metropolitan Life Insurance Company of New York, New
York, NY
Mutual Life Insurance Company of New York (MONY),
New York, NY
Mutual of Omaha, Omaha, NE
New England Life, Boston, MA
The Prudential Insurance Company of America, Newark,
NJ
State Farm Insurance Company, Bloomington, IL
Travelers Insurance Company, Hartford, CT

How to Break into the Field

If you are still in school, check with your school's placement office about insurance recruiters who regularly visit college campuses. Many graduates who are offered employment in the industry make their initial contact with the company during a campus visit by a recruiter. Another suggestion is to check the classified advertisements of your local insurers. Also, don't neglect contacts you might make through summer or part-time work with an insurance company. Several large companies offer internships or have cooperative education agreements with colleges. The best way to find out about them is to write directly to the companies that interest you.

There are also several courses in insurance that you might consider taking. In addition to any offered on your campus, you might want to consider specialized or part-time programs offered by:

The College of Insurance
123 William Street
New York, NY 10038

(This accredited college, supported by the insurance industry and the Insurance Society of New York, offers a nine-month introductory course. It also offers specialized courses in its night division.)

The American College
270 Bryn Mawr Avenue
Bryn Mawr, PA 19010

(This college is responsible for the more than 250 programs across the United States that offer certified life underwriter (C.L.U.) and chartered financial planner (Ch.F.P.) certified programs.)

American Institute for Property and Liability Underwriters
Insurance Institute of America
Providence and Sugartown Roads
Malvern, PA 19355

(This organization administers programs across the United States that offer the chartered property casualty underwriter (C.P.C.U.) designation.)

Professional Insurance Agents
400 North Washington Street
Alexandria, VA 22314

(This professional organization has been offering three-week summer introductory courses in insurance for more than 20 years.)

International Job Opportunities

If you're working for a large insurance company that (1) is doing business overseas; (2) is looking to do business overseas; or (3) has acquired foreign insurance companies, you might find yourself in a position to accept employment overseas. Usually, individuals who speak a foreign language and work as underwriters or sales agents have the best opportunities to be transferred to their firm's foreign offices. Because the American market, especially in health/life insurance, is saturated, insurance companies are looking abroad to increase their sales.

SALES

Responsible for helping to plan their clients' financial security, sales agents are the backbone of the industry. In addition to bringing new business to the company, they often help clients file claims and keep them informed about new or better insurance options. They are also responsible for encouraging the client to renew his or her policy.

The two types of agents are those who work on contract for a small salary, benefits, and commissions for one company, and those who work exclusively on commission for many different insurance companies. The latter are often referred to as brokers or independent agents.

According to the Bureau of Labor Statistics, approximately one of every four agents is self-employed. Some agents specialize in either health/life or casualty/property. Others sell both types of insurance. It is not uncommon for the independent agent to sell real estate or to advise on special financial options—such as annuities or mutual funds—in addition to selling insurance policies.

Agents must be licensed in the state where they sell insurance. Licensing usually requires that the individuals pass a state examination that tests knowledge of insurance principles and state insurance laws.

Qualifications

Personal: Drive. Willingness to work hard to develop a clientele. Good appearance. Self-assurance. Friendly, outgoing, not easily discouraged.

Professional: Excellent oral communications skills. Ability to make sales presentations. Understanding of the personal and financial needs of diverse groups of people.

Career Paths

LEVEL	JOB TITLE	EXPERIENCE NEEDED
Entry	Sales trainee, sales representative	High school diploma; college degree helpful
2	Sales agent	6-18 months
3	Sales manager	3-5 years
4	District manager	5-7 years
5	Regional manager	7-10 years
6	Vice president, sales	10+ years

Job Responsibilities

Entry Level

THE BASICS:Learning about the business of selling insurance. Attending sales strategy sessions as an observer or "tailing" an experienced agent on his or her calls. Assisting established agents to service accounts.

MORE CHALLENGING DUTIES:Making sales calls. Servicing new accounts. Finding and soliciting potential clients.

Moving Up

Successful salespeople often rise quickly in the insurance business. Sales careers can lead to positions as regional, district, and general managers, as well as corporate vice presidencies. In order to move up you must not only show creativity and ability in selling and servicing your accounts, you must also demonstrate your potential as a manager. To move into the corporate structure you must acquire a broad understanding of all functions of the company and of the insurance industry in general.

ACTUARIAL

If salespeople are the backbone of the insurance industry, then actuaries are the brains that make the organization function successfully. These individuals determine premiums and contract provisions of policies. They also calculate the probability of loss due to death, natural phenomenon, sickness, fire, theft, or other catastrophes.

According to the Bureau of Labor Statistics, this profession will see a faster than average growth rate during the 1980s and 1990s. Consequently, many opportunities are available for the individual who strives for challenges and success.

Being an actuary is not a career for anyone with a fear of math. In fact, insurance companies expect actuarial trainees to have been math, business administration, or economics majors and to have taken courses in probability, statistics, and calculus. Computer science course work is a definite plus. Some insurance companies also hire engineering or science majors who have a strong background in mathematics (usually between 20 and 25 credit hours).

Many insurance companies expose their actuary trainees to several of the firm's operations, providing them with a variety of professional experiences. Actuaries may be found in pension planning, group underwriting, investment, or other departments.

An actuary trainee is expected to study for a series of examinations, either individually or through specific courses given by the insurance company or the continuing education division of a nearby college or university. It usually takes between five and ten years to complete the ten examinations, and it is not uncommon for the trainee to study more than 25 hours a week for the examinations. When you have passed all the necessary examinations you become a fellow of the sponsoring organization—either the Society of Actuaries or the Casualty Actuarial Society. This designation marks you as a full-fledged member of the profession, much the same way that passing the bar attests to your professional status as a lawyer. Unlike law, which you cannot practice without passing the bar, you do not need the fellow designation to do the work of an actuary, but you must have it in order to progress in the field. An increasing number of employers hire actuary trainees who have already successfully completed first- and second-level examinations while still in college.

Qualifications

Personal: Patience. Detail-oriented. Ability to work well individually and on a team.

Professional: Strong math and business orientations. Ability to present information in an orderly fashion. Computer skills.

Career Paths

LEVEL	JOB TITLE	EXPERIENCE NEEDED
Entry	Actuary trainee	College degree with strong math background
2	Actuary	1-3 years; at least two professional examinations passed
3	Actuary,	3-5 years; at least five junior associate exams (Society of Actuaries) or seven exams (Casualty Actuarial Society) passed

4	Actuary, associate	5-8 years; six or more exams passed
5	Actuary, new fellow	8-10 years; all ten exams passed
6	Actuary, fellow	10+ years

Job Responsibilities

Entry Level

THE BASICS: Learning how the firm operates through a rotation of training assignments. Working on the simpler actuarial tables. Solving problems contained in them.

MORE CHALLENGING DUTIES: Applying mathematical models to a variety of anticipated health or casualty losses. Designing insurance proposals. Calculating premiums for a new type of insurance. Determining what benefits a policy should contain. Providing statistical information at government hearings on insurance rate changes. Preparing presentations for clients.

Moving Up

It is impossible to progress in this field without passing the examinations given by the Casualty Actuarial Society (for casualty/property insurance) or the Society of Actuaries (health/life insurance). The sooner you attain the title fellow, the sooner you will be ready to enter the managerial ranks. You must also prove your abilities by working on more complex tables and presentations and by being able to arrive at workable solutions to more and more complicated problems. The career opportunities for an actuary are considerable—the presidents of several major insurance companies started their careers as actuaries.

UNDERWRITING

Whereas the sales force acts as the backbone and the actuaries the brains, underwriters are the legs and arms of the organization. They are responsible for determining insurance risk—should Jane Smith or the members of Bill Doe's group be insured, and if so, for how much? What additional risks do these people have? Although underwriters often have a low profile in many insurance companies, their importance cannot be overemphasized. For example, if policies are priced too low, the insurance company could stand to lose money. Similarly, if policies are priced too high, the insurance company could lose business to its competitors.

Most underwriters work in the home offices of their companies. In some organizations, they provide information regarding specific policies to independent or in-house brokers. Advancement often depends on the successful completion of a series of C.P.U.C. (certified property casualty underwriting) examinations. At the entry level a business administration degree is helpful, although many liberal arts majors are hired.

Qualifications

Personal: Ability to work well with others. Patience. Attention to detail and follow-through.

Professional: Aptitude for figures and an understanding of business dynamics.

Career Paths

LEVEL	JOB TITLE	EXPERIENCE NEEDED
Entry	Trainee	College degree
2	Junior Underwriter	1-5 years and continuing education

3	Underwriter	5+ years
4	Underwriting supervisor manager	7+ years
5	Vice president	10+ years

Job Responsibilities

Entry Level

THE BASICS: Evaluating routine applications under the supervision of an experienced underwriter.

MORE CHALLENGING DUTIES: Evaluating applications without supervision. Working on more complex applications.

Moving Up

It will be necessary to earn the fellow designation from the Life Underwriting Training Council in order to move up in this field. Because you will be making decisions about who is to be insured and at what rates, your knowledge must keep up with changes in the industry so that you can make good decisions. With increasing knowledge and experience, you will also be asked to handle larger, more complex groups. Underwriting supervisors frequently write company policy, so a thorough knowledge of company philosophy and procedure will be required before you can move into a managerial or corporate position.

ADDITIONAL INFORMATION

Salaries

SALES
Initially, a small salary ($10,000 to $12,000 a year) plus commissions or other incentive is offered to the tyro salesperson. Later

(the length of time varies depending on the company or agency but can be anywhere from 6 to 30 months), it can be sink or swim with commissions only. Some insurance companies, however, still continue to provide small salaries for their agents. Annual compensation for successful agents can be excellent. For example, life insurance agents with five or more years of experience had a median income of $35,000 a year in 1982. Many agents, especially those who sold casualty policies, earned upwards of $50,000 annually.

ACTUARIAL

Starting salaries for entry-level positions vary, often depending on geographic locations as well as on whether the trainee has already passed any of the three lower-level examinations jointly sponsored by the professional actuary societies. Typical 1982 starting salaries for an actuary trainee, who had not completed any exams, was between $16,000 and $17,000 annually. After successfully passing one examination, an actuary earned between $17,000 and $18,500 a year, after passing two examinations, between $18,500 and $20,000 a year.

Depending on the number of professional examinations completed, salaries rise appreciably. For example, average annual salaries of new associates of both actuary societies was between $24,000 and $28,000 in 1982. Actuaries who became fellows in that same year had yearly salaries between $35,000 and $45,000. Fellows with additional experience are known to earn upwards of $50,000 annually.

UNDERWRITING

A salary survey conducted by several property and liability insurance companies found that the median salary for underwriters in 1982 was $18,500 a year. Senior underwriters working with personal lines of insurance had median annual salaries of $21,000 in comparison to commercial line underwriters who earned $23,700. Supervisors in property and liability companies had incomes between $26,500 and $28,000 a year.

Working Conditions

Hours: Expect work weeks of between 35 and 40 hours, depending on the firm. Overtime is usually not mandatory for underwriters and actuaries except during certain busy periods.

For sales agents who have passed the training period, things are a bit different. Often they make their own hours, scheduling appointments around a client's time schedule. This can mean night and weekend hours as well as more than the usual 35-to-40-hour work week.

Environment: The quality of work space varies greatly, depending on the number of people in the office. Don't expect your own office as a newcomer. More than likely you'll have to share space bullpen-style with co-workers. Private offices usually go to more senior staff members.

Workstyle: Better get used to working at your desk. With the exception of sales agents, who must interact with clients in their homes or places of business, individuals working in the insurance industry perform many of their tasks on computer terminals, typewriters, and other office equipment located adjacent to their desks.

Travel: In general there is little travel at the entry level, except locally. Agents usually see their clients outside the office. Underwriters and actuaries sometimes travel to branch offices. Associate and senior-level employees attend industrywide conferences and seminars.

Extracurricular Activities/Work Experience

Serving as club treasurer

Working on fund-raising drives

Student membership in professional organizations

Part-time or summer jobs in sales, in the benefits/personnel departments of corporations or in insurance companies.

Internships

Many companies offer internships and cooperative work-study arrangements. No single directory lists all these opportunities, but your school placement service can be of assistance. You can also write directly to the personnel departments of companies that interest you.

Recommended Reading

BOOKS

Glossary of Insurance Terms by Thomas E. Green, Robert W. Osler, and John S. Bickley, The Merrit Company: 1980

The Insurance Almanac, Underwriting Publishing Company: 1982

Insurance Facts, Insurance Information Institute: 1983

Life Insurance Factbook, American Council of Life Insurance: 1983

Principles of Insurance (7th edition) by Robert I. Mehr and Emerson Cammack, Richard D. Irwin, Inc.: 1980

Principles of Insurance by George E. Rejda, Scott, Foresman: 1982

PERIODICALS

Best's Review (monthly), A.M. Best Company, Inc., Ambest Road, Oldwick, NJ 08858

Business Insurance (biweekly), Crain Communications, 740 North Rust Street, Chicago IL 60611

Insurance Careers (annual), Resort Managements, Inc., P.O. Box 4169, Memphis, TN 38104

Life Insurance Selling (monthly), Commerce Publishing Company, 408 Olive Street, St. Louis, MO 63102

National Underwriter (weekly), National Underwriter Company, One Marine View Plaza, Hoboken, NJ 07030

Professional Agent (monthly), Professional Insurance Agents, 400 North Washington Street, Alexandria, VA 22314

Today's Insurance Woman (quarterly), National Association of Insurance Women, P.O. Box 4410, Tulsa, OK 74159

(For a comprehensive guide to insurance periodicals, check the *Insurance Periodicals Index,* issued annually by the Special Libraries Association and NLS Publishing Company.)

Professional Associations

American Council of Life Insurance
1850 K Street, N.W.
Washington, DC 20006

American Institute for Property and Liability Underwriters
Insurance Institute of America
Providence and Sugartown Roads
Malvern, PA 19355

American Insurance Association
85 John Street
New York, NY 10038

American Society for Chartered Life Underwriters
270 Bryn Mawr Avenue
Bryn Mawr, PA 19010

Casualty Actuarial Society
One Penn Plaza
New York, NY 10001

Independent Insurance Agent of America, Inc.
85 John Street
New York, NY 10038

Insurance Information Institute
110 William Street
New York, NY 10038

Insurance Library, The College of Insurance
123 William Street
New York, NY 10038

Insurance Library Association of Boston
156 State Street
Boston, MA 02109

Life Underwriting Training Council
1922 F Street, N.W.
Washington, DC 20006

National Association of Casualty and Surety Agents
5225 Wisconsin Avenue, N.W.
Washington, DC 20015

National Association of Independent Insurances
2600 River Road
Des Plaines, IL 60018

National Association of Insurance Women
P.O. Box 4410
Tulsa, OK 74159

National Association of Life Underwiters
1922 F Street, N.W.
Washington, DC 20006

Professional Insurance Agents
400 North Washington Street
Alexandria, BA 22314

Risk and Insurance Management Society, Inc.
205 East 42nd Street
New York, NY 10017

Society of Actuaries
500 Park Boulevard
Ataska, IL 60143

Society of Chartered Property and Casualty Underwriters
Kahler and Hall
Providence Road
Malvern, PA 19355

INTERVIEWS

Maria Leon, Age 25
Analyst
Royal Insurance Company, New York, NY

Unlike many analysts and underwriters, I did not have a liberal arts
background. In fact, I knew when I was planning for college that I
wanted a career in insurance and wanted to remain in New York
City. Therefore, I chose the College of Insurance and participated
in their five-year co-op program and earned a B.B.A. degree in
business administration.

This co-op program enabled me to work on a part-time basis
with Royal. I would go to school for a semester and work the

following semester. Royal paid two-thirds of my tuition during college semesters and a regular salary when I worked there in alternate semesters. The experience was great—I was able to work in the international, marketing, claims, and underwriting departments.

As a full-time analyst with Royal for the past one and a half years, I work closely with underwriters. I have earned my C.P.C.U. (casualty property certified underwriter) designation, the same as any underwriter would. This is similar to an advanced degree and increases knowledge as well as the value of the underwriter to the organization.

And just what does an analyst do? Basically, I service the underwriters. This means I present them with research data-specific industry reports, or even new information about different types of insurance, and help them compare and select risks. Normally we'll write a company manual that details what the underwriters should look for when determining rates and risks.

In the research capacity, one of my responsibilities is to keep track of legislation in my insurance area—commercial lines. What changes in California vehicle laws might make for a better risk, or under what circumstances a policy may be cancelled—this is the type of information I collect.

During a typical day I'll work on short- as well as long-term research projects, and I'll often take calls from branch offices regarding procedures and forms in addition to answering some underwriting questions. Sometimes someone in the branch office will ask for an endorsement (a change in policy) to cover a special situation. What I'll do is try to phrase it correctly and then pass it along to our legal department. If it's acceptable, I'll notify the individual in the branch.

It is not uncommon for an analyst to travel to branch offices for research. Last year I spent some time in our Atlanta, GA, office, looking through their automobile underwriting files. This research gave me a better perspective on what actually was happening in the marketplace, and this is the type of information that would influence future policy changes or rate hikes.

Gil Goetz, Age 26
Underwriter
Kemper Group, New York, NY

After I graduated from Ohio Wesleyan University in 1980 with a degree in economics, I decided to take advantage of an opportunity to learn insurance brokering in London, England. There, I became a broker trainee. I returned to the United States within a year.

I had heard about Kemper's underwriting training program and wanted to become an underwriter, so I applied and was accepted as a trainee. My training included spending a month at the Kemper home office in Long Grove, IL, where I received excellent, intensive training.

As a casualty underwriter, I represent the company to brokers and agents. I answer questions about policies and often recommend the policies that might be best for a client's needs. I also service these policies, which means that I provide the brokers with the information they need to attract and maintain business.

I also examine potential insureds. In examining these accounts, it is essential that the underwriter look at inspection reports and research. For example, if a broker calls and wants to know what rate we will charge to insure a large manufacturing plant, I'll look at an inspection report made out by an engineer and at other data available about the type of work done at the plant. If an underwriter underestimates the risk, the insurance company stands to lose money; if the risk is overestimated, the client will take its business elsewhere.

We're using computers more and more in our operations. If a broker calls, we can check to see if premiums are still outstanding for the client and find what endorsements might have been made. You are on the telephone a lot in this job. You have to know where to find information and be able to provide it quickly.

I enjoy working with people, and I like the feeling that I am providing a service to society. I get a lot of satisfaction out of doing my job.

MARKET RESEARCH

IN ancient times, people flocked to star-gazers and oracles to ask about the future. Today predictions are made by market researchers, who try to foresee if a particular group—consumers, businesspeople, voters—will believe in a product, a business decision, a candidate, or an idea. Rather than consulting the stars or relying on their instincts, market researchers base their predictions on research. They spend days, weeks, months, and even years sampling opinions, tastes, and reactions.

Many variables besides quality account for success or failure in the marketplace—changing tastes and trends, public perceptions (and misconceptions), subliminal messages. Before a new product appears in the stores, before an old favorite gets new packaging, even before a product is discontinued, market research is conducted and its conclusions incorporated into business strategies and advertising campaigns.

Food processors and manufacturers of cosmetics and consumer goods need to know who will buy a certain product and why, what kind of packaging is most enticing and appropriate, how much consumers are willing to pay, and how frequently consumers will use the product. To find the answers, new products are tested against established ones, facsimiles of the product are test-marketed, and surveys of potential consumers are made. The results may confirm a company's conviction that a sufficient market for a given product exists or that it is the right time to introduce such a product. Market researchers often suggest pricing and marketing strategies based on consumer responses.

Research may be concerned with something other than a consumer product. Current issues, the ramifications of business decisions, and even political campaigns are studied through market research. Regardless of the subject, all research follows a similar pattern—the problem is defined, a research strategy is developed, information is collected and analyzed, and the results are interpreted and presented to the users. Information may be gleaned from phone interviews, on-the-scene impromptu interviews with a target group (e.g., moviegoers, shoppers), written surveys or focus groups, the carefully selected people who fit the demographics of the client's intended market.

Two different types of work go into market research: data collection and information analysis. Data collection is the more detailed. It involves tallying questionnaires, conducting phone interviews, and assembling relevant printed information. Much of the research is either quantitative or qualitative. Quantitative research tends to produce numbers-oriented studies; qualitative reports feature more subjective information, such as opinion sampling. Information analysis is more sophisticated work; it involves interpreting the results of the research and writing up conclusions in a report or presentation for the client. There is also tedious number-crunching work, which is given to the least experienced people. But computers are eliminating the drudgery of such work and, best of all, drastically reducing the amount of time needed to do complicated cross-tabulations.

Some companies do both information collection and analysis, but market research firms often rely on tabulation services and field services to perform the time-consuming tasks that precede analysis. Tabulation services specialize in collecting data of any sort, usually through surveys and questionnaires supplied by the research company. They do not analyze the data, they simply collect it. Field services perform a more personalized aspect of the same task. They specialize in interviews that take many forms: with groups, with individuals, by phone, or in shopping centers. These companies may tabulate the results for their clients.

Market research is a growing field that is extending its influence into businesses of all kinds and to hospitals, colleges, and other nonprofit organizations that need to know how to manage their own development, who their constituency is or ought to be, and, often most important, how to target potential contributions and successfully solicit donations.

No one specific academic background is required for a job in market research, but you must be able to work effectively and comfortably with numbers and to articulate your ideas clearly and convincingly. Although an undergraduate degree is all you'll need to get an entry-level position, you should be prepared to take some graduate courses if you want to make your career in this field. Although you don't have to be a math major to do quantitative research, you will probably feel more comfortable in that area if you have a strong background in math or statistics. After you gain some experience and demonstrate your ability to grasp quickly what kind of research is necessary in any particular client situation, you should be able to move up into a challenging position.

Job Outlook

Job Openings Will Grow: Faster than average

Competition for Jobs: Keen

New Job Opportunities: Expansion in the industry is taking place in research companies—independent firms that offer research services to clients. As new service industries, such as the newly expanding banking industry and cable television, continue to enter the marketplace, the need for research companies will grow.

Geographic Job Index

New York, NY, and Chicago, IL, are the leading centers of market research, but job opportunities exist across the country, mostly—but not exclusively—in urban areas.

Who the Employers Are

MARKET RESEARCH FIRMS perform complete research studies, although they may use outside tabulation houses and field services for data collection. Once they receive the data, they analyze and report on the data to their clients. They may also initiate their own research projects and then sell the findings to interested companies. Research companies often specialize in a single type of client. As a result, many firms have staffs of fewer than ten people.

CONSUMER GOODS MANUFACTURING FIRMS often have market research departments within their corporate structure. These departments may or may not carry out numerical research, but they design the research projects that need to be done, analyze and interpret the results, and make recommendations based on their conclusions. Usually, only a handful of people are employed in-house, and most of the jobs there go to experienced people.

Major Employers

A.C. Nielsen Company, Northbend, IL
Arbitron Ratings Company, New York, NY
Audits & Surveys, New York, NY
Burke Marketing Services, Cincinnati, OH
IMS International, New York, NY
Market Facts, Chicago, IL
Marketing and Research Counselors, Dallas, TX
NFO Research, Toledo, OH
NPD Group, Port Washington, NY
Sellings Areas-Marketing, Inc., New York, NY

How to Break into the Field

You'll stand a better chance of getting hired in an entry-level job if you have related experience. Field services employ large numbers of high school and undergraduate students in part-time and summer positions, usually as interviewers who call people across the country to ask prepared questions and take responses.

Large firms (those with 40 employees or more) occasionally recruit on campus, but, in general, you will have to investigate openings on your own. Firms are listed in the Yellow Pages under "Marketing Services." Newspaper help-wanted ads normally advertise positions for experienced personnel only. But it's often worthwhile to contact the company that is advertising the job on the chance that the new senior-level person may need an assistant.

The Chemical Marketing Research Association runs a yearly three- or four-day course in July. It's titled Basic Chemical Marketing Research Short Course, but it is a good introduction to the market research process in general. For information, contact the Chemical Marketing Research Association. (Address given at the end of this chapter.)

International Job Opportunities

Market research is done in most Western countries, but international job opportunities are very limited, since most positions are filled by nationals.

RESEARCH ANALYSIS

The entry-level position in research analysis is the junior or associate analyst. You will assist experienced analysts by handling the routine detail work that accompanies all projects. In firms or departments that do field work, you may begin by interviewing or editing and coding—checking to see that all questionnaires are completed and assigning numerical codes to nonnumerical responses so that results can be tabulated. Firms that depend on field services may send new employees to a service for a few weeks so they can get a firsthand understanding of the information-gathering process.

Typically, one analyst is responsible for each project. Besides preparing and presenting the conclusions of a study, this individual must coordinate the efforts of all contributors—one or more junior analysts and field and tabulation personnel. Analysts, especially those in senior or executive positions, may solicit new business and maintain contacts with past clients.

To become a successful market research analyst, you must be able to (1) read a qualitative report and determine what questions need to be asked to get concrete, quantitative answers; (2) produce a logical, coherent picture from the results of a numerical survey or the varied answers of an opinion poll; and (3) communicate effectively, guiding your clients to conclusions that are appropriate to the results of your research, convincing them that your recommendations are well-grounded and credible. Deadline pressure is constant; the entire process of research and analysis often takes no longer than six to ten weeks. You may work on one project at a time or be concerned with several in various stages, and you're sure to have assignments changed suddenly.

Qualifications

Personal: Good judgment. Able to communicate clearly. Personable appearance and manner. Good powers of concentration. Ability to work on a team. Problem-solving mentality.

Professional: Strong writing and communications skills. Math and statistical know-how. Good phone manner. Typing or word processing skills.

Career Paths

LEVEL	JOB TITLE	EXPERIENCE NEEDED
Entry	Coder-editor, junior or associate analyst	College degree
2	Analyst	1-2 years
3	Senior analyst, research manager	4-7 years
4	Market research director	7+ years

Job Responsibilities

Entry Level

THE BASICS: Clerical duties: typing, filing, handling the flow of correspondence. Proofreading questionnaires. Writing cover letters, memos, and progress reports. Organizing completed studies and reports.

MORE CHALLENGING DUTIES: Writing questionnaires, using successful examples. Basic data analysis. Organizing and rearranging tables, charts, and raw data. Writing introductions and reports for coders and interviewers.

Moving Up

The key to success in this competitive business is building an understanding of the research process as quickly as possible. You must demonstrate the ability to study data and apply your conclusions to specific problems. You will not deal directly with the users of the research until you have adequate experience (a year or more). At first, you will meet with brand managers, gathering background information and drafting initial proposals. This work will provide an understanding of user needs. As a researcher handling your own projects, you will respond to these needs through your analyses. A good deal of writing and speaking is involved, and you must be both candid and diplomatic in the way you present results.

ADDITIONAL INFORMATION

Salaries

Each year, the American Marketing Association conducts a salary survey of its members. The average annual salaries for market research personnel nationwide in the 1983 report were:

Analyst	$24,128
Manager or supervisor	$32,945
Director	$41,361
President	$53,483

Working Conditions

Hours: The standard 40-hour week can stretch to 12-hour days and include weekends in times of heavy business. But there are corresponding slack periods. Hours tend to be more regular in the larger research firms and in-house departments.

Environment: Analysts often have their own small offices, and most research firms have at least one larger conference room where analysts will get together to discuss ongoing projects.

Workstyle: The work day is hectic for both entry-level and senior personnel. The junior analyst generally spends each day in the office. Analysts visit clients and potential clients. Research often involves a great deal of phone work.

Travel: Opportunities for national and international travel exist at many research firms. Although field services can provide coverage of virtually any location in the United States, an analyst may occasionally travel to supervise research for an international corporation on market conditions in another part of the globe, or to investigate personally a locale's unique characteristics.

Extracurricular Activities/Work Experience

Business Research Practicum

American Marketing Association—student member

Canvassing/phone interviewing for charities or political campaigns

Campus newspaper—reporting

Internships

There are no formal internship programs in market research, but you can try to set one up on your own by contacting the personnel director in some of the larger companies.

Recommended Reading

PERIODICALS

Careers in Industrial Marketing Research published by The Chemical Marketing Research Association (free)

Careers in Marketing by Neil Hobart, American Marketing Association, Monograph Series #4 (free)

Employment and Career Opportunities in Marketing Research published by the Marketing Research Association, Inc. (free)

Marketing Communications (monthly), United Business Publications, 475 Park Avenue South, New York, NY 10016

The Marketing News (biweekly), American Marketing Association, 222 South Riverside Plaza, Chicago, IL 60606

Marketing Times (bimonthly), Sales and Marketing Executives International, 330 West 42nd Street, New York, NY 10036

Professional Associations

American Marketing Association
250 South Wacker Drive
Chicago, IL 60606

The Chemical Marketing Research Association
139 Chestnut Avenue
Staten Island, NY 10305

The Life Insurance Marketing Research Association
170 Sigourney Street
Hartford, CT 06105

INTERVIEWS

Tom Keels, Age 29
Research Director
Louis Harris Associates
New York, NY

I got into market research in 1980. After working in publicity at a publishing house, I decided to switch careers. I knew I liked marketing, so I looked at advertising, marketing consulting, and market research. A friend was working at a small research company called Crossely Surveys; he helped me get a part-time job as an editor-coder so I could see if I liked the work. I found it interesting, so when I was offered a job as a project assistant a few months later, I accepted.

I started in an entry-level job because very few skills transfer directly from publicity to market research. I had good writing skills and was comfortable talking on the phone, but these were not important immediately because I wasn't in a position to deal with clients.

As a project assistant I carried out the mechanical details of a particular job. In other words, I made sure the questionnaires were typed, proofed, and sent out to the field. I supervised some interviewing and oversaw editing, coding, and computer cross-tabulation. I remember very clearly one of the first projects I worked on. The client was a major manufacturer of baked goods. We wanted to see if the quality of the packaging could be enhanced, made more attention-getting, by widening the border of the brand-name logo by one-quarter of an inch. A complex scheme was devised in which people were shown slides of new and old packaging in quick succession. If they noticed the new border, we knew it would be a success. Having no idea of what to expect, I was sent to shopping malls to grab shoppers and ask them to look at slides of a cookie package! It was an interesting introduction to research!

The initial excitement of gathering data tends to wear off once you learn basic research techniques. The process is the same whatever product you are investigating. The challenge lies in the analysis, not the actual research.

After a year at Crossely, I moved to AMF, another research company, as project director. I started dealing with clients, usually counterparts at my level; that is, people managing, rather than planning, a study. In mid-1982, I joined Louis Harris Associates as a research associate and was named research director in early 1983. I'm still overseeing detail work—that's something you really can't avoid even when you reach the level of vice president—but I have more creative input. At the end of a study I analyze data, meet with clients to go over results, and write a final report.

I now do a lot of work with banks. The creation of the "financial supermarket" has make the banking industry more conscious of the marketplace. As a result, I've had to learn a lot about finance. Banking is one area where research is just beginning to make inroads, and it's exciting to sell potential clients on the importance of research itself, not just the result of a particular study.

I like the variety that comes from working with a research supplier. You have to be a good juggler because you may be dealing with seven or eight projects at once. I like sitting down with seemingly unrelated data and creating a logical picture from them. But this analysis is interspersed with going out to meet people and sell them on a survey idea. It's not all desk work and it's not all sales; it's a combination of the two. Research provides a chance to use different parts of myself in different ways.

John DeBiassio, Age 35
Vice President
Russell Research
New York, NY

Although I've worked in market research for seven years, my association with it goes back much farther. Before I came to

Russell Research I worked in straight marketing with Progresso Foods. I started at Progresso, working in product management, after getting a master's in business administration. Eventually I became marketing services manager, and in this position I began to get involved with research. The last position I held at Progresso was assistant director of marketing; my functions included being research director. We never conducted any research of our own, but I worked with the research companies who researched the market for us.

I made the switch to market research for a number of reasons. Most of all, I find research fascinating. I also like the fast pace of a research company; it's much more active than straight marketing. The diversity of products to be dealt with was another strong attraction.

My marketing experience has been a valuable factor in my success in research. I came to this profession with a pragmatic approach that resulted from understanding marketing needs. I see beyond the research techniques. This results-oriented viewpoint improves my dealings with clients; I've been in their place and understand their goals.

I've worked on a wide variety of projects, from the simple to the complex. I've tested very specific promotional and advertising materials, such as a tag on clothing. Small details can make a difference in the way the public responds to a product. You must ask: what is the effectiveness of a colored tag versus a black and white one? Of one brand name over another? I've also handled much broader problems—evaluating entire marketing strategies, determining the best packaging, repositioning product lines. Here the questions require more analysis. Does the product live up to consumer expectations? Can it be sold to a specific segment of the market?

A complex project I've worked on was a tourism study for a country that hopes to attract American tourists. The study involved a series of questions: How do Americans perceive this country? Does the country have an image problem in the United States? If so, is it a major problem? How can it be overcome?

Often the results of a particular study show there is a problem—in packaging, advertising, marketing, whatever. Unfortunately, not all clients take this news and our advice as well as we would like. Some will request further research to confirm our findings. Of course, this in never the case when the study has favorable results!

SECURITIES

FORTY million people and institutions in the United States alone trade in stocks and bonds. A report on the day's trading, the Dow-Jones Index, is a staple of the evening news broadcast. The business of selling securities is a large and lucrative one; top brokers and analysts earn as much as $400,000 a year. It's easy to see, then, why so many success-oriented people set their sights on "Wall Street"—a term that long ago came to mean the securities industry as a whole.

The term, of course, derives from the handsome, beaux arts-style building at 11 Wall Street that is the home of the New York Stock Exchange and is linked by half a million miles of telephone and telegraph wires to brokerage offices around the world. This vast communications network enables a buyer in London, England, for example, to purchase stock from a seller in California in a matter of minutes.

There are 6,935 brokerage firms in the United States registered with the Securities and Exchange Commission. Ranging in size from small, two-room operations to multinational giants like Merrill Lynch, they can be found in cities across the country and around the world. New York, NY, however, is the undisputed capital of the securities industry, offering more job opportunities than anyplace else.

But although the New York Stock Exchange, or "Big Board," is by far the largest central marketplace in the United States for securities trading, it's not the only one. The American Exchange is located nearby, and there are several regional exchanges: the Pacific, in San Francisco, CA, the Midwest, in Chicago, IL, and others in Boston, MA, Cincinnati, OH, and Philadelphia, PA.

Not every stock can qualify to be listed on one or more of the country's exchanges (requirements for the New York exchange are the most rigorous). Stocks are traded by brokers who are members of the exchange on which the stock is listed. (A brokerage house may be—and often is—a member of more than one exchange.)

When a broker receives a call from a client who wishes to buy a particular stock, the purchase order is directed to the floor of the appropriate exchange via computer. The brokerage firm has a representative there, called a floor broker. Every listed stock has a trading post, which is a specific location on the exchange's floor, and the floor broker goes there to ask for a "quote"—both the highest open bid made for the stock and the lowest available offer. Based on the quote, the broker offers a price, shouting out his or her bid for the number of shares the client wants. A floor broker with shares of that stock to sell calls out an offer to sell at the offered price, and a trade is made. The transaction is recorded immediately and the price of the stock is sent back to the broker's office by computer; the broker in turn relays the information to the client. The order is also sent over the wires and appears on the ticker tape in the office of every firm with a seat on that exchange.

Unlisted stocks are traded "over the counter." The broker can call up on an electronic visual display unit information listing the securities firms that trade in the various unlisted stocks, and the trade is then conducted directly by telephone.

Securities firms are currently locked in fierce competition with banks for customers' dollars. Recent federal deregulation permits both of these industries to offer products and services that were once the exclusive domain of the other. This means that a broker, in addition to selling stocks and bonds, may now offer clients an array of such products and services as asset management accounts, which pool all a client's assets into a single account. Checks may then be written against the consolidated account. The intense competition between brokers and bankers has resulted in converting many clients who were simple savers into investors.

Computers are revolutionizing the securities industry: speeding information from analysts to brokers, making possible complex computations that take some of the guesswork out of forecasting, and providing a host of other services that have eliminated much drudgery for the research department and enabled brokers to expedite their clients' orders. Analysts are using microcomputers to analyze balance sheets and cash flow and give brokers fast answers to clients' questions.

Now when a client calls a broker to learn the import of a company's $15 million increase in sales, for example, the analyst can punch the figure into the computer and be back to the broker in seconds with the answer. With the time the computer saves, countless more calculations can be performed in a day. Analysts can also look farther into the future, forecasting earnings three or four years ahead by trying out many different scenarios on the computer, whereas previously earnings were forecast for only a year ahead. And analysts are using the computer's word processing capabilities to produce research reports, complete with computer-drawn graphics, that can go right to the printer, eliminating the need for a typist or artist. When a stock is faltering, the broker can use the word processing capability to write individual letters to every client who holds the stock, recommending a call to the broker to discuss alternative investments.

Virtually every broker, no matter what the size of the firm, uses a microcomputer to store information on a client's holdings. This data may be cross-referenced in a variety of useful ways: by stock, by industry, or by investment objective, for example. Some firms are creating computer programs relating to options and bond trading that will balance the potential risks and gains in a proposed deal for a particular client.

Job categories in the securities field are:

- **Sales**
- **Research**
- **Operations**

The most prestigious and best-paying jobs are in sales and research. Sales requires high energy, excellent judgment, and, increasingly, some selling experience, and research requires sharp analytical skills (and more often than not an M.B.A.). Because the failure rate for recent college graduates entering the securities sales field with no relevant experience is extraordinarily high (some studies say it runs close to 95 percent) many firms now will only hire sales trainees who are at least 26 years old and have had some sales experience.

If you lack an M.B.A. degree or sales experience but are bent on a career in securities, an alternative for you might be the operations department—the "back office," where all the firm's transactions are processed. When sales slots open up, many firms fill them with the best and brightest from their operations department.

Job Outlook

Job Openings Will Grow: Faster than average

Competition for Jobs: Keen

There are about 15,000 security analysts in the United States, compared with more than 80,000 brokers (and their ranks keep growing), making sales a considerably easier area to crack—assuming you have the required sales experience.

New Job Opportunities: The deregulation of the banking industry, the peak performances of the stock market in recent times, and the dizzying array of new options being made available to investors are creating new job opportunities in both sales and research.

Deregulation has paved the way for companies to buy up a variety of financial services and bring them all under one roof to create a "financial supermarket." The first to do so was Sears, Roebuck & Company: at more than 125 Sears store locations, customers can now make deposits at Allstate Savings & Loans, purchase insurance at Allstate Insurance, buy real estate through Coldwell Banker, and purchase securities through Dean Witter Reynolds. More than 850 new brokers were hired in 1983 to work in these Sears store locations, and brokers will continue to be added as more Sears stores open financial supermarkets. J.C. Penney has since followed Sears's lead.

The fierce competition for investors' money is spurring brokerage houses to enlarge their sales and research departments to attract customers, creating more jobs for brokers and analysts.

Geographic Job Index

New York, NY, has the highest concentration of brokerage firms of any city in the United States, and most of the major firms are headquartered there, so it's the best place to find jobs in research and operations. Other cities with a high concentration of brokerage firms include Boston, MA, Philadelphia, PA, Chicago, IL, Dallas, TX, San Francisco, CA, and Los Angeles, CA. The major firms have an extensive network of branch offices (Dean Witter Reynolds, for example, has more than 325 branch offices throughout the 50 states), and even small cities have one or more brokerage offices. So you could find a job in sales almost anywhere in the country, although the field is larger, naturally, in a big city.

Who the Employers Are

NATIONAL BROKERAGE FIRMS   employ thousands of employees in their nationwide branch offices. The biggest of them all, Merrill Lynch, employs more than 15,000 people. These firms maintain large research departments and spend millions of dollars each year tracking down the most attractive investments for their customers.

REGIONAL BROKERAGE FIRMS provide many of the same services offered by national firms but specialize in trading and promoting the interests of local companies. They employ fewer people than national firms in their offices (all of which are concentrated in their immediate area). Some very small brokerage firms have one office in one city only.

DISCOUNT BROKERAGE HOUSES are firms that do nothing but execute trades. They do not maintain research departments or offer advice, and their fees to investors are correspondingly lower. Many banks are forming partnerships with discount brokers so they can offer their customers discount brokerage services. Two such partnerships are Bank of America and Charles Schwab and Chase Manhattan Bank and Rose & Company. Many discount brokerage houses are national, but there are local ones as well.

COMMERCIAL BANKS have clients that are principally institutions and individuals with large sums to invest. They employ portfolio managers to handle such investments. Their staffs also include buy-side analysts, who offer purchase recommendations. (Unlike sell-side analysts, who are at securities firms that sell stock, buy-side analysts work for institutions making stock purchases.)

INSURANCE COMPANIES hire buy-side analysts also, who are responsible for advising the company about investing the huge sums of money collected as premiums from policyholders.

Major Employers

Allen & Company, New York, NY
Bear Stearns & Company, New York, NY
A.G. Becker, Inc., New York, NY
Dean Witter Reynolds, Inc., New York, NY
Donaldson Lufkin & Jenrette, Inc., New York, NY
Drexel Burnham Lambert, Inc., New York, NY
A.G. Edwards & Sons, St. Louis, MO
The First Boston Corporation, New York, NY
Goldman Sachs, New York, NY
E.F. Hutton Company, New York, NY
Kidder Peabody Company, Inc., New York, NY
Merrill Lynch Pierce Fenner & Smith, Inc., New York, NY
Morgan Stanley & Company, New York, NY
Paine Webber, New York, NY
Prudential-Bache Securities Brokers, New York, NY
L.F. Rothschild Unterberg Towbin, New York, NY
Salomon Brothers, Inc., New York, NY
The Securities Groups, New York, NY
Shearson Lehman/American Express, Inc., New York, NY
Shelby Cullom Davis & Company, New York, NY
Smith Barney Harris Upham & Company, Inc., New York, NY
Spear Leeds & Kellogg, New York, NY
Stephens, Inc., Little Rock, AR
Thomson McKinnon Securities, New York, NY

How to Break into the Field

Because the securities industry is one in which the professionals tend to know their colleagues, the surest route to a job interview is through personal contacts—your school's alumni, family friends, neighbors, a relative's stockbroker. Failing that, try a letter-writing campaign: If you'd like a job as a broker write to the account executive recruitment office at the headquarters or to the branch manager at locations in your area. If your interest lies in operations, write to the operations manager at the firm's headquarters. Send a carefully worded letter stating your qualifications and requesting an interview. Enclose your résumé. Follow it up with a phone call requesting an appointment for an interview.

International Job Opportunities

Extremely limited. Most of the major firms have offices abroad, but they tend to hire local residents for the positions that exist there.

SALES

Brokers (also known as account executives, registered representatives, or salespeople) act as agents for people buying or selling securities. Because the performance of an account executive is crucial to the client's satisfaction and the firm's reputation, candidates are put through a rugged qualifying process at any large brokerage firm. The first hurdle is usually a general aptitude test; if you complete that successfully, you'll be interviewed by a succession of people, usually beginning with a corporate recruiter or a branch manager, who will rate your potential for success as a broker. The final hurdle will be a measurement of your sales skills in a test that includes exercises simulating problems and situations commonly faced by brokers. These involve telephone calls to prospects and relevant analytical work. Try to talk to a broker beforehand to prepare for this phase of the process.

As a beginning broker, your aim will be to build up a clientele. The best place to start is with people you know—family, friends, neighbors, members of groups or clubs to which you belong. You'll also be combing phone directories and mailing lists for names of prospective clients and spending the bulk of each day soliciting (many firms expect new brokers to make between 50 and

100 phone calls a day). While you continue to search for new business you'll be servicing your clients: keeping them abreast of their stocks' performance, executing trades, and recommending financial investments suitable to their needs and objectives.

Brokers usually specialize in one type of security, either stocks or bonds, and also either in retail sales, where your clients are individuals, or institutional sales. In addition, there are floor brokers, who work on the floor of a stock exchange, executing the actual trades of listed stocks.

To become a broker, you must pass the licensing exam given by the New York Stock Exchange, the main regulatory body for all the exchanges; in order to take the test, you must be sponsored by a firm. The firm that hires you will put you through an intensive account executive training program and give you study guides to help you prepare for the licensing exam. During the first three months of your training, while you prepare for the exam, you'll be observing the activities of a working brokerage firm. An additional month might be spent taking courses at the firm's training center.

During the next year, you'll be a broker-in-training at a branch office, with the manager of the branch serving as your supervisor. While you're in training, you'll be paid a salary. Once the training period ends, however, you'll be working strictly on commission, so your income will depend on how many transactions you process. Because brokerage firms demand a high level of productivity (many expect to see brokers earn about $50,000 in gross commission the first year), be prepared to work hard.

Qualifications

Personal: Self-confidence. Personality. Foresight. Drive. Persistence. Ability to influence others. The strength to withstand frequent rejection.

Professional: Ability to work comfortably with numbers. Understanding of basic business concepts. Previous sales experience preferred.

Career Paths

LEVEL	JOB TITLE	EXPERIENCE NEEDED
Entry	Sales trainee	College degree, sales experience helpful
2	Account executive	1-3 years
3	Branch manager	4-6 years
4	Regional manager	6-10 years
5	National sales manager	10+ years

Job Responsibilities

Entry Level

THE BASICS: Identifying prospective clients through mailing lists and phone directories and making cold telephone solicitations. Answering clients' telephone queries. Reading financial publications. Processing transactions.

MORE CHALLENGING DUTIES: Advising clients on appropriate investment strategies. Keeping current clients informed of their stocks' performance by telephone or letter. Studying reports from the research department.

Moving Up

Your success depends on how hard you're willing to work—the number and quality of clients you can attract, your investment acumen, the soundness of the judgments you make on the basis of factual material from the research department, and your willingness to do more than simply take orders from your clients. It takes years to build a reputation as a broker who knows his or her business thoroughly. If you become a top performer in your branch and have managerial know-how, you may be offered the job of branch manager.

If you reach that point, you'll be required to relinquish all but a few of your clients. (You may be able to retain those with whom you have a personal relationship or who are your biggest investors.) As a branch manager, you'll be paid a salary plus a bonus based on the amount of money the branch office brings in. In addition, you will collect commissions on any transactions you continue to make.

RESEARCH

A broker is only as successful as the company's research department. Knowing which stocks to go after and which to sell comes from listening to the presentations and reading the reports of the firm's researchers, or security analysts, who study stocks and bonds, assess their current value, and forecast their earning potential. Security analysts tend to specialize in a single industry, such as oil or steel, and quickly becoming experts in their area. Most security analyst jobs go to candidates who have an M.B.A. However, some brokerage firms will hire recent college graduates on the condition that they attend business school at night, and will offer tuition reimbursement.

Qualifications

Personal: Ability to work under pressure. Foresight. Self-confidence. Ability to trust your own instincts.

Professional: Verbal and writing skills. Keen analytical skills. Familiarity with accounting procedures. Ability to read between the lines of annual reports. Facility working with a software "calc" program.

Career Paths

LEVEL	JOB TITLE	EXPERIENCE NEEDED
Entry	Research assistant/ junior analyst	M.B.A. degree helpful
2	Senior analyst	3 + years
3	Managing director	10 years

Job Responsibilities

Entry Level

THE BASICS: Reading financial reports. Analyzing corporate balance sheets. Working with figures. Making written recommendations to more senior analysts. Assisting senior people at whatever research work needs to be done.

MORE CHALLENGING DUTIES: Accompanying senior analysts on visits to corporation officials to gather firsthand information about the company. Advising the firm's brokers on specific stocks. Fielding questions posed by brokers.

Moving Up

After three or more years of gaining familiarity with and expertise in a particular industry, if you demonstrate that your analyses and interpretations of trends and developments are sound, you may be promoted to senior analyst. As a senior analyst, you'll be called on to answer any difficult questions posed by brokers or their clients, and act as adviser on all stocks related to the industry in which you are expert. You'll periodically visit branch offices to deliver oral presentations, accompanied by written reports, on your industry to brokers there. You'll also be accompanying institutional salespeople on their visits to lucrative accounts.

OPERATIONS

The operations department, or "back office," is where the hundreds of thousands of daily transactions made by the firm's brokers are processed and recorded. The work is divided among several groups of clerks, each group with specific responsibilities. The purchasing and sales clerks make sure that every buy matches up with a sale by studying the computer printouts that record all transactions. The main source of this information is the Securities Industry Automation Corporation, an automated clearinghouse that is jointly owned by the New York and American exchanges. The printouts show every buy and sale on these exchanges in a single day; in addition, this same source provides information on national trading. Firms trading on exchanges outside New York, NY, receive comparable information from other automated sources. If the firm has made a buy and no corresponding sale appears on the printout, then a recording error has been made, and the purchasing and sales clerks must call around to other securities firms to try to learn who made the sale. Clerks in client services post dividends to clients' accounts and mail out monthly statements. Margin clerks keep track of clients' accounts, making sure they haven't purchased more on credit than is legally allowed. Compliance clerks ensure that transactions are completed according to all rules and regulations spelled out in the *New York Stock Exchange Constitution and Rules* book. Department heads oversee each of these services.

Securities are received and stored or transferred in a top-security area called the cage, where only a few people in the firm are allowed to enter. Cage clerks microfilm all securities and box them for storage in the vault or transfer them elsewhere to be stored.

Qualifications

Personal: Conscientiousness. Good powers of concentration. An eye for detail.

Professional: An understanding of basic business concepts. An affinity for and ability to deal with numbers.

Career Paths

LEVEL	JOB TITLE	EXPERIENCE NEEDED
Entry	Clerk	College degree helpful
2	Supervisor	2-3 years or an M.B.A. degree
3	Section head	4-5 years
4	Manager	6+ years

Job Responsibilities

Entry Level

THE BASICS: Checking printouts. Balancing sales and buys. Answering telephones. Microfilming and storing stock certificates. Mailing out monthly statements. Filing.

MORE CHALLENGING DUTIES: Fielding brokers' questions. Managing a greater workload as your speed and efficiency increase.

Moving Up

An accomplished clerk may be promoted to a supervisory position. As a supervisor you're typically responsible for five to seven clerks, assigning their work, monitoring their productivity, and offering guidance when needed. You will also do some administrative work, such as submitting absentee reports, preparing productivity reports for upper management, and establishing vacation schedules. A section head acts as liaison between departments and is prepared to deal with problems that may arise in day-to-day operation so that the department functions smoothly and effectively.

ADDITIONAL INFORMATION

Salaries

SALES commissions vary with the type of security and the size of the transaction. Retail brokers collect between 30 and 40 percent of the fee that the firm charges for each transaction; institutional brokers collect somewhat less—around 15 percent—because large blocks of securities are being traded. For brokers who bring in a high volume of business, there are numerous incentives, such as free trips and raises in commission. The income potential is unlimited, and some brokers gross in excess of $1 million a year in commissions.

RESEARCH salaries range from $30,000 a year for entry-level M.B.A.s to six-figure incomes for managing directors. The analysts are rated by the brokers on the basis of the quality and depth of their research and their record of success. These ratings are carefully considered when analysts are up for their biannual bonuses.

OPERATIONS salaries for clerks range from $9,000 to $20,000 a year, plus overtime, depending on experience. Salaries for supervisors with M.B.A. degrees start at $30,000 a year, plus bonuses.

Working Conditions

Hours: A broker's day usually begins at 8 A.M., in time to read the papers and financial journals and talk with the research department before the exchanges open at nine. Brokers often leave the office once trading ends at 4 P.M. Operations work is usually nine to five, with overtime when trading is heavy. Supervisors and section heads put in slightly longer hours, perhaps eight-thirty to six, to catch up with administrative details or attend meetings. Research analysts work the longest hours, typically past 7 P.M.

Environment: Junior brokers, clerks, and junior analysts work in bullpen arrangements. Senior brokers, operations managers, and senior analysts have private offices. Typically, those in sales enjoy the plushest surroundings.

Workstyle: Sales personnel spend a great deal of time on the phone, either speaking with established clients or soliciting new business. Institutional salespeople may wine and dine big clients after normal business hours. Clerks and operations supervisors spend nearly all their time on paperwork, but operations managers may be in meetings up to half of each day. Research is also a desk job; the study of financial statements involves using the microcomputer to arrive at various indicators of a company's financial status: asset/debt ratio, sales/inventory ratio, sales/debt ratio. You will meet at least once a week with other members of your research team.

Travel: Opportunities to travel are nonexistent for brokers and operations staffs. Regional and national sales managers visit branch offices frequently. As a research analyst, how much you travel and how far you go depends on the industry you cover. If you specialize in an industry the center of which is in your home area, out-of-town trips may be infrequent.

Extracurricular Activities/Work Experience

Team sports—participating as a member or leader

Investment clubs—participating as a member

Sales experience—working in sales of any kind; telephone solicitation work a plus

Internships

Internships are not easily arranged in the securities industry. Your best bet might be to apply to small, local brokers; however, any prospective sponsor of an internship will expect to see a solid academic record.

Recommended Reading

BOOKS

The Money Game by Adam Smith, Vintage: 1976

The Money Messiahs by Norman King, Coward-McCann: 1983

Stealing from the Rich: The Story of the Swindle of the Century by David McClintick, Quill Publications: 1983

DIRECTORIES

Broker-Dealer Directory (annual), Securities and Exchange Commission, Washington, DC

Security Dealers of North America (semiannual), Standard & Poor's, New York, NY

Who's Who in the Securities Industry (annual), Economist Publishing Company, Chicago, IL

PERIODICALS

Barron's (weekly), Dow Jones & Company, 22 Cortlandt Street, New York, NY 10007

Business Week (weekly), McGraw-Hill, Inc., 1221 Avenue of the Americas, New York, NY 10020

Dun's Business Month (monthly), Dun & Bradstreet Corporation, 875 Third Avenue, New York, NY 10022

Financial World (bimonthly), Macro Communications, Inc., 1250 Broadway, New York, NY 10001

Forbes (biweekly), 60 Fifth Avenue, New York, NY 10011

Fortune (biweekly), Time-Life Building, Rockefeller Center, New York, NY 10020

Institutional Investor (monthly), 488 Madison Avenue, New York, NY 10022

Investment Dealers Digest (weekly), 150 Broadway, New York, NY 10038

Money (monthly), Time-Life Building, Rockefeller Center, New York, NY 10020

The Wall Street Journal (daily), Dow Jones & Company, 22 Cortlandt Street, New York, NY 10007

Weekly Bond Buyer (weekly), 1 State Street Plaza, New York, NY 10004

Professional Associations

Financial Analyst Federation
1633 Broadway
New York, NY 10019

National Association of Security Dealers
2 World Trade Center
New York, NY 10048

Securities Industry Association
120 Broadway
New York, NY 10271

INTERVIEWS

Assistant Vice President, Research
L.F. Rothschild Unterberg Tobin, New York, NY

I was a triple in college—history, political science, and economics—and I hasten to add that I managed to do that major in economics without taking any courses in mathematics. I definitely did fall into that category of women who have a negative reaction to numbers. Upon graduation I worked for the Corporation for Public Broadcasting in their human resources development. Part of my responsibility was monitoring the employment and portrayal of women and minorities in public broadcasting. That necessitated doing quarterly reports to a congressional committee, and I had to start compiling employment figures, statistics—and there was math staring at me! I later became responsible for the departmental budget, which was rather substantial as our department was responsible for handing out training grants throughout the system. I quickly discovered there was nothing to be frightened about.

I enjoyed that for a while, but got somewhat tired of the nonprofit orientation. It's not very insightful, but the way I ended up in securities was to look in Washington, DC, and to find out what kind of private oriented enterprises there were. And there were not many. I won't say "securities" bounced right out of the phone book—but it was the only industry I could see getting into without a great deal of difficulty. I had invested with some success on my own and found it interesting, so I investigated the various brokerage firms in Washington, and found that Ferris and Company, which is a fine regional house in Washington, had a superior, intensive training program.

Once I was in securities I found out that if I wanted to go beyond the basic retail broker status, I had to have a graduate degree. And that's why I went back to school to get an M.B.A. I went to George Washington University while I was still working at Ferris. Because the only management position available at a regional house would be a branch manager, and that certainly was out of the question with my few years of experience, and not having built and enormous clientele book, I decided to come back to New York, which is my native state.

I never liked pure sales and never did cold calling, and quite frankly was uncomfortable with pure commission as a source of income. So I found myself getting more and more involved in the total financial picture of my clients, which gave me a greater level of security in terms of what I was or was not doing with their money. And that was quite suitable experience for the posiion I now hold in Rothschild's research department. I'm in what's known as portfolio research, and that job entails essentially being a broker to our brokers. They submit their client portfolio with the appropriate investment objective information, and we analyze the portfolio or develop a portfolio to meet the client's needs. The beauty of this is that it gives the client excellent service, because this is done at no additonal fee, and I have no vested interest in whether the broker buys or sells. I make decisions on a needs basis for the client versus a need basis for the broker.

The bottom line about having the M.B.A. is that it helped me get the job. I don't know that I use more that 10 percent of what I learned. The program that I was involved in was more qualitative than quantitative, which I frankly liked, and I think an awful lot of large corporations are coming to the conclusion that the quantitative programs are great in the short term, but they're finding that the long-term objectives of many corporations are being sacrificed. That's a consideration one should look at seriously when picking an M.B.A. program. I also think one should work before going for a graduate degree. Although there are hordes of recruiters on campuses these days, and M.B.A.s are still pulling in a fairly nice salary for an initial job, I do think that the allure of the degree without work experience is rapidly dissipating. More and more employers are saying that without experience what you've learned means nothing to you because you haven't been able to apply it while you learned it. The M.B.A. was more a premium degree when I got it than it is today, but it's a question of having the degree to get the door open now.

Sixty to 70 percent of my day is spent talking to brokers, responding to questions on particular stocks about whether they're appropriate for specific clients, looking at portfolios, and going to meetings with other analysts to look at companies or to discuss the general market outlook. The balance of the time is spent with my clients, which is the icing on the cake. I enjoy my salary compensation, and then can do as much commission business as I want. I'm constantly reading research reports of other firms or independent research organizations, and company annual reports, and doing spread sheets on earnings projections. I also function as a conduit between the specialized analysts who cover specific industries and the broker for those securities that our firms covers on a regular basis. When we're talking about companies that are not regularly followed, that's when I have to look at them.

I like the sense of power in this job. It's really rather heady to have brokers who've been on Wall Street for 30 years have to ask me if it's okay to by or sell something. But I also enjoy the research end. I have found—much to my surprise over the years—that numbers are not intimidating at all. It gives me the opportunity to be both a broker for those clients that I do handle without being compelled to trade in their accounts to make my living. And I like being of assistance to the brokers because, although I don't have a vested interest in whether they buy or sell, over the long term if you do a portfolio structure that is appropriate for their client they keep the client. It's not a question of perhaps buying one or two stocks that don't turn out so the client goes to some other broker. If you can do a total picture so that no single security will make or break them, they're going to keep their portfolio with you.

Leah Pfeffer
Administrative Manager, Institutional Sales
Dean Witter Reynolds, Inc., New York, NY

My first profession was teaching—I have a B.S. and an M.S. in education—but after three years at the head of a third-grade classroom, I was ready for something new. I was interested in business (and I must admit I was ready to work with adults), but beyond that I didn't have a clear idea of where to start looking. An employment agency sent me to interview for a position as a sales assistant with a brokerage house. I knew little about either securities or sales, but the job interested me and it met my two basic requirements—it didn't require typing and I wouldn't be taking a cut in pay by switching jobs. I didn't get that job, but I found what I had been looking for. I applied for other sales assistant openings and wound up at Thomson McKinnon. That was in 1968.

I learned a great deal about securities. The firm sent me to the New York Institute of Finance, which prepared me to take (and pass) the registered representative exam with the New York Stock Exchange. But I knew I didn't want to be an assistant forever. I pursued sales, moving to a small brokerage house called Hirsch and Company. Few woman were in sales at that time. In fact, I have wondered if the primary reason I got that job was because I was interviewed by one ot the few female partners then in the business.

I received no formal training—I was given a phone and a desk, and I was on my own! Building a client base was tough. I found myself in a bear market with few products to sell. At the time, brokers dealt mainly with stocks. We sold some bonds, but the options market was really just starting. Today, a broker has much more to work with.

The bad part of being a broker is that you are always on the job. Wherever you go, whomever you meet, one thing is foremost in your mind—making client contacts. I did a lot of cold calling. I did hit on a trick to make contacts, however. I would go through the phone book, calling everyone with the name of Pfeffer. By playing up the coincidence of our names, I could break the ice, and often people would talk to me because of the connection.

The firm went out of business, which gave me a chance to reevaluate my goals. I came to the conclusion that I would be happier not selling. I was not bad at selling, but the job just didn't fit my personality. I went back to Loeb Rhoades (now a part of Shearson Lehman/American Express), handling day-to-day, administrative details as a supervisor. After four years, I moved to Bache Halsey Stuart, Inc. (now Prudential Bache), where I spent another four years as manager of marketing and support services in the institutional sales department.

In institutional sales, we sell our product—our research—to major clients, such as bank trust departments and large pension funds. I was responsible for discovering what our clients needed in terms of the research itself and what they expected in terms of its presentation. Some wanted a broad analysis; others asked for more specific information. The data must be easily understandable and, above all, must be timely.

I left Bache after four years, moving to Dean Witter Reynolds. I still work with institutional sales, but am more involved with overseeing department functions. Institutional sales is now getting into new areas. Electronic transmittal of data is speeding our delivery to customers. And we are now looking into closed circuit television. With it, we will be able to contact our clients directly; our research analysts and salespeople won't travel, but may make all their analytical presentations and sales calls on television. Your clients always expect you to have a crystal ball. Not so long ago, clients wanted forecasts for the coming year or two; now they want predictions five years in advance! As research techniques become more sophisticated, our forecasts seem to be getting much more accurate, but of course room for error remains.

Although I do not do actual selling, my sales background has helped me immensely. I understand the pressures on our salespeople. And in a sense, I still do some selling—not to the clients, but to the salespeople. I tell them what we can supply to clients, and I motivate them to sell our services.

I am a member of the Financial Women's Association of New York, an organization that includes women from many different financially oriented professions. I enjoy meeting other professional women to compare notes and exchange information. And, as you progress in your career, networking is important.

I have also supplemented work experience with an M.B.A. I went at night, taking six years to complete the degree. As you can tell, I wasn't in a hurry! The best place to learn is on the job, but I felt I needed the M.B.A. to remain competitive. So far, having the degree has not made a difference in my job; however, if I decide to look for another job, it may be valuable. The M.B.A. is simply becoming more common. In order to compete against other advanced-degree holders, you need it.

BIBLIOGRAPHY

The College Graduate's Career Guide by Robert Ginn, Jr., Charles Scribner's Sons: 1981

College Placement Annual by the College Placement Council: revised annually (available in most campus placement offices)

The Complete Job-Search Handbook: All the Skills You Need to Get Any Job and Have a Good Time Doing It by Howard Figler, Holt, Rinehart & Winston: 1981

Consider Your Options: Business Opportunities for Liberal Arts Graduates by Christine A. Gould, Association of American Colleges: 1983 (free)

Go Hire Yourself an Employer by Richard K. Irish, Doubleday & Company: 1977

The Hidden Job Market for the 80's by Tom Jackson and Davidyne Mayleas, Times Books: 1981

Jobs for English Majors and Other Smart People by John L. Munschauer, Peterson's Guides: 1982

Job Hunting with Employment Agencies by Eve Gowdey, Barron's Educational Series: 1978

Making It Big in the City by Peggy J. Schmidt, Coward-McCann: 1983

Making It on Your First Job by Peggy J. Schmidt, Avon Books: 1981

National Directory of Addresses and Telephone Numbers, Concord Reference Books: revised annually

The National Job-Finding Guide by Heinz Uhrich and J. Robert Connor, Doubleday & Company: 1981

The Perfect Résumé by Tom Jackson, Doubleday & Company: 1981

Put Your Degree to Work: A Career Planning and Job Hunting Guide for the New Professional by Marcia R. Fox, W.W. Norton: 1979

The Student Entrepreneur's Guide by Brett M. Kingston, Ten Speed Press: 1980

What Color Is Your Parachute? A Practical Manual for Job Hunters and Career Changers by Richard N. Bolles, Ten Speed Press: 1983

Where Are the Jobs? by John D. Erdlen and Donald H. Sweet, Harcourt Brace Jovanovich: 1982

INDEX

NOTES

NOTES

NOTES

NOTES

NOTES